NOV 0 5 2009

WITHDRAWN FROM LIBRARY

SCYTHIANS and SARMATIANS

BARBARIANS!
SCYTHIANS and SARMATIANS

KATHRYN HINDS

MARSHALL CAVENDISH · BENCHMARK · NEW YORK

To Alena, with love and pride

The author and publisher specially wish to thank Dr. Jeannine Davis-Kimball, of the Center for the Study of Eurasian Nomads, for her invaluable help in reviewing the manuscript of this book.

Marshall Cavendish Benchmark 99 White Plains Road Tarrytown, New York 10591
www.marshallcavendish.us
Text copyright © 2010 by Marshall Cavendish Corporation Map copyright © 2010 by Mike Reagan

All rights reserved. No part of this book may be reproduced or utilized in any form or by any means electronic or mechanical including photocopying, recording, or by any information storage and retrieval system, without permission from the copyright holders.

All Internet sites were available and accurate when this book was sent to press.

LIBRARY OF CONGRESS CATALOGING-IN-PUBLICATION DATA
Hinds, Kathryn, 1962-
Scythians and Sarmatians / by Kathryn Hinds. p. cm. — (Barbarians!) Includes bibliographical references and index.
Summary: "A history of the Scythians and Sarmatians, horse-riding nomads of Eurasia, who lived contemporaneously with the ancient Greeks and Romans" —Provided by publisher. ISBN 978-0-7614-4072-7
1. Scythians—History—Juvenile literature. 2. Sarmatians—History—Juvenile literature. 3. Nomads—Eurasia—History—Juvenile literature. 4. Horses—Eurasia—History—Juvenile literature. 5. Eurasia—History—Juvenile literature.
6. Eurasia—Ethnic relations—Juvenile literature. I. Title. DK34.S4H56 2010 939'.51—dc22 2009016496

EDITOR: Joyce Stanton PUBLISHER: Michelle Bisson ART DIRECTOR: Anahid Hamparian SERIES DESIGNER: Michael Nelson

Images provided by Debbie Needleman, Picture Researcher, Portsmouth, NH from the following sources: *Front cover:* Horsemen from the Steppes (gouache on paper) by English School (20thc). Private Collection/©Look and Learn/The Bridgeman Art Library. *Back Cover:* Belt Buckle from the Siberian collection of Peter I (gold) by Scythian (7thc. BC). Hermitage, St. Petersburg, Russia/The Bridgeman Art Library. *Page i:* Horse nomad (silver gilt) by Scythian (7thc. BC). Private Collection/Photo ©Boltin Picture Library/The Bridgeman Art Library; *pages ii-iii:* ©akg-images, London/Russian State Museum, St. Petersburg; *page 6:* ©The Trustees of the British Museum. All rights reserved; *page 8:* Helmet with combat scenes (detail), 4th c. gold from Perederiieva Mohyla (Kurhan 2) Museum of Historic Treasures of the Ukraine, Kiev. ©Bruce M. White photograph courtesy of The Walters Art Museum; *page 10:* akg-images, London/Coll. Archiv f.Kunst & Geschichte, Berlin; *page 12:* National Gallery, London/The Bridgeman Art Library/Getty Images; *pages 13, 49:* akg-images, London/Museo della Civiltà Romana, Rome; *page 14:* akg-images, London/Badisches Landesmuseum, Karlsruhe; *page 17:* Two archers (gold) by Scythian (4thc. BC). Private Collection/ Photo ©Boltin Picture Library/The Bridgeman Art Library; *page 18:* The Art Archive/Gianni Dagli Orti; *page 20:* Plaque: Panther curved round. Gold; cast, chased. 10.9x9.3cm. Sakae Culture. 7th-6thc. BC. Inv.no. Si-1727.1/88. The State Hermitage Museum, St. Petersburg. Photograph ©The State Hermitage Museum; *page 21:* Queen Tomyris, from the Villa Carducci series of famous men and women, c. 1450 (fresco) by Castagno, Andrea del (1423-57). Galleria degli Uffizi, Florence, Italy/The Bridgeman Art Library; *page 22:* ©Araldo de Luca/CORBIS; *page 27:* Mask for a horse head. Felt, leather and gold. 20x60x40cm. Pazyryk Culture. 5thc. BC. Inv. No. 1295/238. The State Hermitage Museum, St. Petersburg. Photograph ©The State Hermitage Museum; *page 28:* Plaque depicting two Scythians sharing a drink (gold) by Scythian (4thc. BC). Private Collection/Photo ©Boltin Picture Library/The Bridgeman Art Library; *page 30:* ©Werner Forman/Art Resource, NY. Private Collection, New York, NY; *page 31:* ©SISSE BRIMBERG/The State Hermitage Museum, St.Petersburg/National Geographic Image Collection; *page 33:* Pin with warrior holding a head (bronze) by Scythian. Private Collection/Photo ©Boltin Picture Library/The Bridgeman Art Library; *page 34:* ©gezmen/Alamy; *page 35:* ©Sisse Brimberg/National Geographic/Getty Images; *page 37:* Mummy of a Chieftain with a loincloth. Wool; 1.180 cm. Pazyryk Culture. 5th-4thc. BC. Inv. No. 1687/89. The State Hermitage Museum, St. Petersburg. Photograph ©The State Hermitage Museum; *page 38:* Amazon mounted on the edge of a mixing bowl. Western Greek or Etruscan from Capua, c. 480 BC (bronze). British Museum, London, UK/The Bridgeman Art Library; *page 39:* The Art Archive/Natural Science Academy Kiev/Alfredo Dagli Orti; *page 41:* ©SISSE BRIMBERG/Museum of Historic Treasures of the Ukraine, Kiev/National Geographic Image Collection; *page 43:* ©Werner Forman/Art Resource, NY. The State Hermitage Museum, St. Petersburg; *page 44:* ©The London Art Archive/Alamy; *page 46:* akg-images, London/Musée du Louvre, Paris; *page 47:* Belt Buckle from the Siberian collection of Peter I (gold) by Scythian (7thc. BC). Hermitage, St. Petersburg, Russia/The Bridgeman Art Library; *page 52:* ©Art Media/Heritage/The Image Works; *page 54:* The Beheading of German Nobles, detail from the Column of Marcus Aurelius (Colonna Antonina). 180-196 AD (marble) by Roman. Piazza Colonna, Rome, Italy/Alinari/The Brigeman Art Library; *page 57:* Bildarchiv Preussischer Kulturbesitz/Art Resource, NY. Musei Capitolini, Rome Italy; *page 59:* ©Vanni/Art Resource, NY. Museo della Civilta Romana, Rome, Italy; *page 60:* ©Peter Horree/Alamy; *page 63:* ©Guy Edwardes Photography/Alamy; *page 64:* akg-images, London/Lobdengaumuseum, Ladenburg; *pages 67, 68:* The Art Archive/The State Hermitage Museum St. Petersburg/Alfredo Dagli Orti; *page 69 (top and bottom):* ©Luka Mjeda/Art Resource, NY. Museum of Historic Treasures of the Ukraine, Kiev.

Printed in Malaysia
135642

front cover: The Scythians' mastery of mounted archery made them a formidable force in the ancient world.
half-title page: A seventh-century BCE Scythian plaque of gilded silver portrays a helmeted man in riding posture—a position in which the dead were often buried.
title page: After using their bows and arrows to attack from a distance, Scythian warriors close in with spears and shields.
page 6: From a plate made in Athens, Greece, around 500 BCE, an archer, dressed and armed like a Scythian, blows a battle trumpet. Greek archers learned their skill from Scythian mercenaries hired by Athens, and many seem to have adopted Scythian clothing.
back cover: This gold belt buckle weighs more than a pound; it was one of a pair worn together as a sign of a noble warrior's power.

CONTENTS

WHO WERE THE BARBARIANS?	6
1. Introducing the Scythians and Sarmatians	9
2. Persian Problems	19
3. Life and Death on the Steppe	29
4. Peoples on the Move	43
5. Enemies and Allies	55
KEY DATES IN SCYTHIAN AND SARMATIAN HISTORY	68
GLOSSARY	70
FOR MORE INFORMATION	71
SELECTED BIBLIOGRAPHY	72
SOURCES FOR QUOTATIONS	73
INDEX	76

Who Were the Barbarians?

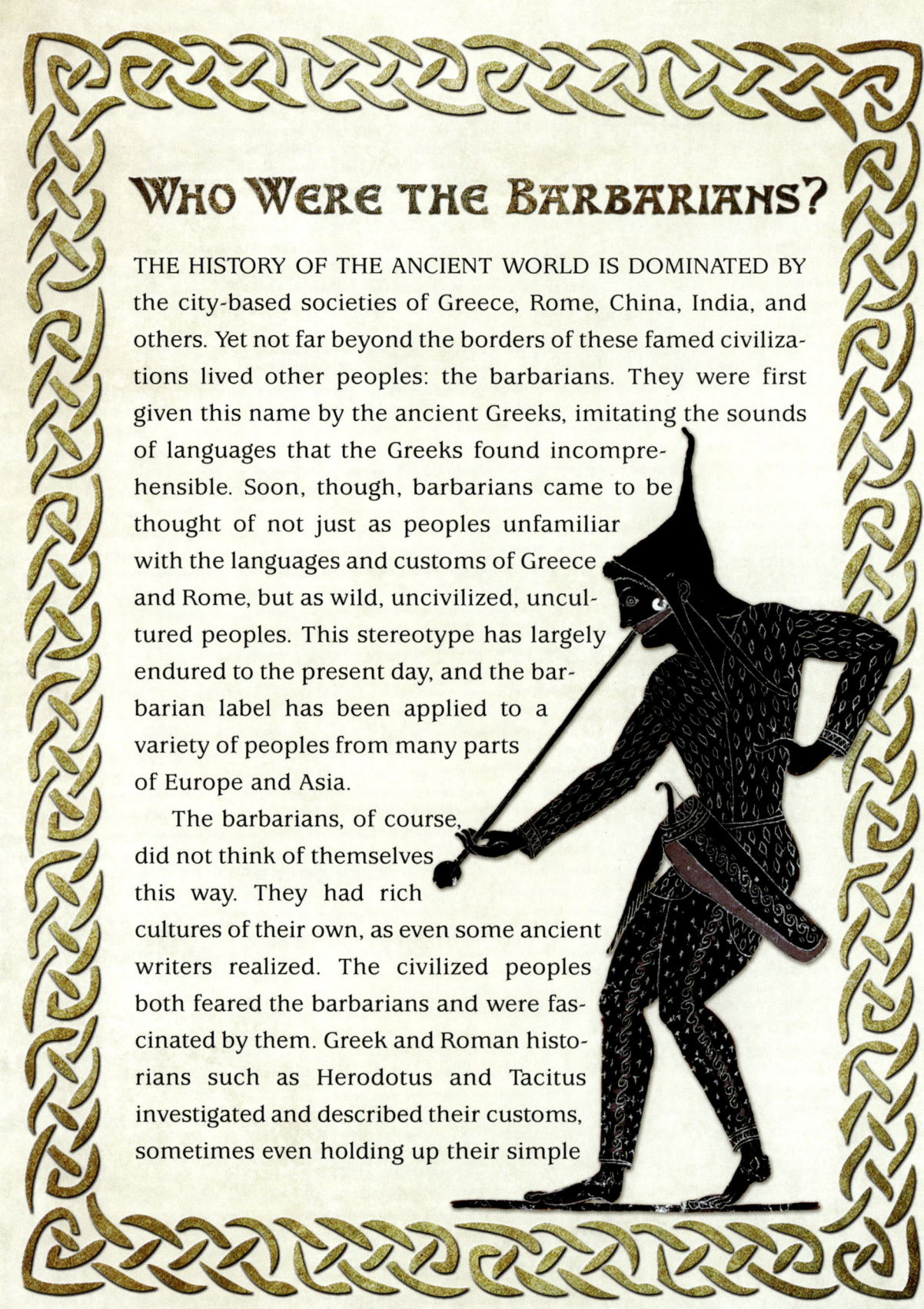

THE HISTORY OF THE ANCIENT WORLD IS DOMINATED BY the city-based societies of Greece, Rome, China, India, and others. Yet not far beyond the borders of these famed civilizations lived other peoples: the barbarians. They were first given this name by the ancient Greeks, imitating the sounds of languages that the Greeks found incomprehensible. Soon, though, barbarians came to be thought of not just as peoples unfamiliar with the languages and customs of Greece and Rome, but as wild, uncivilized, uncultured peoples. This stereotype has largely endured to the present day, and the barbarian label has been applied to a variety of peoples from many parts of Europe and Asia.

The barbarians, of course, did not think of themselves this way. They had rich cultures of their own, as even some ancient writers realized. The civilized peoples both feared the barbarians and were fascinated by them. Greek and Roman historians such as Herodotus and Tacitus investigated and described their customs, sometimes even holding up their simple values as a lesson for their own, more sophisticated societies. Moreover, the relationships between the barbarians and civilization were varied and complex. Barbarians are most famous for raiding and invading, and these were certainly among their activities. But often the barbarians were peaceable neighbors and close allies, trading with the great cities and even serving them as soldiers and contributing to their societies in other ways.

Our information about the barbarians comes from a variety of sources: archaeology, language studies, ancient and medieval historians, and comparisons with later peoples who lived in similar conditions. Unfortunately, though, we have almost no records in the barbarians' own words, since many of these peoples did not leave much written material. Instead we frequently learn about them from the writings of civilizations who thought of them as strange and usually inferior, and often as enemies. But modern scholars, like detectives, have been sifting through the evidence to learn more and more about these peoples and the compelling roles they have played in the history of Europe, Asia, and even Africa. Now it's our turn to look beyond the borders of the familiar civilizations of the past and meet the barbarians.

> A variety of systems of dating have been used by different cultures throughout history. Many historians now prefer to use BCE (Before Common Era) and CE (Common Era) instead of BC (Before Christ) and AD (Anno Domini), out of respect for the diversity of the world's peoples.

INTRODUCING the SCYTHIANS and SARMATIANS

IN 9 CE THE ROMAN POET OVID ARRIVED IN TOMIS, A TOWN ON the coast of the Black Sea. Ovid had been banished there by the emperor Augustus, for reasons that have never been clear. Back in Rome, Ovid had been celebrated and successful. But Tomis was a rustic outpost, an old Greek colony now occupied largely by barbarians called Getans. The townspeople didn't even speak Latin, the language of Rome—none of them could understand, let alone appreciate, Ovid's poetry. To make matters worse, Tomis lay close to lands occupied by the Sarmatians, who raided the town and surrounding countryside frighteningly often.

Banishment could not keep Ovid from writing poetry. His previous works had been about love and mythological marvels, but now he wrote of his sorrows and fears. As a major source of those fears, the Sarmatians show up over and over in the poems Ovid composed during his exile, as in this passage:

Opposite page: A Scythian warrior, bow case hanging from his belt, raises his spear to defend a fallen comrade. This image is part of the decoration on a helmet made from a single sheet of gold.

Would you like to know just how things are
In Tomis town and how we live?
Though Greek and Getan mingle on this coast
It owes more to the Getan than the Greek.
Great hordes of them and their Sarmatian
Cousins canter to and fro along the rough roads,
Everyone with bow and quiverful of
Arrows, yellow-nibbed and vile with venom.
Villainy of voice and face betray their thoughts;
Hairiness of head and beard tell us they
Have never seen a barber.

Ovid may have been miserable in Tomis, but out of his misfortunes came vivid depictions of the Sarmatians. His poems help bring to life for us a people who had no form of writing of their own. They themselves left behind only their art and their graves. These, together with the reports of Ovid and others, show us that the Sarmatians shared in a nomadic lifestyle and horse-riding culture that stretched back more than six hundred years. Before the Sarmatians, the northern Black Sea coast had been home to the Scythians, another group of nomads. Both were among the many related peoples whose horses thundered across the plains of Asia and Europe, disturbing the peace of the settled farmers and city dwellers of the ancient Middle East, Greece, and Rome.

Ovid, one of ancient Rome's greatest writers, who turned even the sorrows of exile into poetry

SHEPHERDS OF THE STEPPE

From eastern Europe to eastern China stretches a band of grasslands, the Eurasian steppes. In some places the terrain is perfectly flat; in others there are rolling hills. Parts of the steppe are very dry. There are also many areas where rivers and streams bring enough moisture to the land to support farming, and trees grow along the waterways. South of the steppe lie deserts, mountains, or seacoast. In the north the grassy steppe edges into what is called forest-steppe, mixed woodlands and meadows.

Today much of the steppe is farmland, thanks largely to modern equipment that makes it easy to cut through the dense sod and work the heavy black soil. But when a German writer visited the steppe in 1841, he traveled across a sea of grass virtually unchanged since ancient times:

> One sees nothing but wormwood and more wormwood, then nothing but vetch . . . then half a mile of mullein and another half of melilot, then an expanse of swaying milkweed, a thousand million nodding heads, then sage and lavender for the duration of an afternoon doze, then tulips as far as the eye can see, a bed of mignonette two miles across, whole valleys of caraway and curled mint, endless hills covered in resurrection plant and six days' journey with nothing but dried-up grass.

Thousands of years ago, these plains and the nearby woodlands and mountains were home to abundant wildlife: deer, elk, boar, wolves, tigers, snow leopards, hawks, eagles, and more. One animal, though, became the basis of an entire way of life: the horse. Steppe peoples began raising domestic horses for meat, milk, and hides at least four thousand years ago. Eventually they also started using horses to pull carts and wagons. Then, roughly three thousand years ago, they mastered the art of horseback riding. This gave them the ability to cross great distances at great speed. From the height of horseback, they could see far over the tall grasses. When hunting, they could chase down their quarry more easily. When herding their livestock—sheep, cattle, and horses—they could

An 1859 painting by French artist Eugène Delacroix depicts Scythians riding, relaxing, and milking a mare on steppeland along the Black Sea.

take them deeper into the steppe to graze and could round them up efficiently. They were able to handle much larger flocks and herds, too.

With the mastery of horsemanship, steppe peoples were no longer limited to the area right around their river-valley farms. The steppe offered plenty of room for expanding herds. And when all the grass was eaten or dried-up in one area, the horse enabled people to drive their animals to fresh pastures. These factors led many groups of steppe dwellers to embrace the mobile lifestyle known as nomadic pastoralism. *Nomadic* refers to traveling or wandering, and *pastoralism* means caring for livestock.

The steppe nomads' travels were not aimless wanderings. They had fairly regular routes they followed, moving from one area to another based on the availability of water and grass at different seasons. Sometimes one group's routes crossed another's, which could be a source of conflict. When a tribe's population grew, its herds had to grow, too, and they would expand the territory they traveled and claim new pastures.* Since these might already be claimed by other nomads, such expansion was another factor that led to conflict.

As steppe peoples fought to protect their herds and their grazing lands, they developed a distinctive and extremely effective method of

---

*This might be a slow process. Population would begin to grow when the tribe adopted the typical nomad high-protein diet (mainly meat, milk, and cheese), but in some areas of the steppe it was centuries before the population pressure resulted in expansion.

warfare: mounted archery. They used a short, powerful bow that was easy to manipulate while on horseback (unlike the longbows that we are familiar with from images of Robin Hood, for example). The nomads drew and shot their arrows rapidly, skillfully aiming not only to the front and to the side but also twisting to shoot at enemies behind them—all at full gallop. They kept their hands free for archery by controlling their horses completely with knees and calves.

A Sarmatian archer's horse gallops ahead as he turns to shoot at pursuing Roman soldiers. This image was sculpted in Rome in 113 CE to commemorate a battle that took place about ten years earlier.

The nomads' military skills made them masters not only of the steppe but of the settled communities in the river valleys and forest-steppe. Nomads needed these communities to supply them with grain and other produce, along with wood, metals, and various manufactured goods. The nomads could trade for these things, since the settled peoples often needed livestock, leather, and other animal products. But the nomads could also use their superior strength to take what they wanted—raiding was an important part of the nomad economy and lifestyle.

The fact that settlements on or near the steppe were so vulnerable to raids also gave nomads the opportunity to collect tribute from them. The basic understanding was, *You give our tribe grain and supplies, and we'll protect you from other tribes who might want to attack you. Plus we won't attack you, either.* The majority of town and village dwellers were unwarlike farmers and craftspeople, but among the nomads nearly all men (and often a number of women) were trained and capable warriors. So it usually seemed like a better idea to give the nomads what they wanted rather than try to fight them should they come to take it by force.

EARLY ENCOUNTERS

Among the earliest nomad horse archers described by ancient historians were people whom the Greeks called Scythians. The Scythians may

THE REAL CENTAURS

GREEK TRADERS PROBABLY CAME INTO CONTACT WITH THE SCYTHIANS NEAR THE BLACK Sea in the late eighth century BCE. The first Greek author to mention them was Hesiod, who wrote of "mare-milking Scythians" around 700 BCE. This description highlights the nomads' dependence on their horses not only for transportation but also for food. Their staple drink was koumiss—fermented, slightly alcoholic mares' milk. They ate horsemeat (in addition to other kinds of meat), especially at funeral and religious feasts. In emergencies they even drank horse blood (from a small cut in the neck, which did not seriously harm the animal). They also depended on horses for raw materials such as horsehide, horsehair, hoofs, and bone.

Steppe nomads began learning to ride before they began to walk; by the age of three they were skilled riders. Adults were so comfortable and accomplished on horseback that they must have seemed to be at one with the animal. The Scythians barely even used reins to control their mounts, most of the time riding with their hands free. They also tended to sit forward on the horse, often crouching over the neck in a way similar to how modern jockeys ride. When the Greeks first encountered these people who appeared to be completely joined to their horses, it is no wonder they developed legends about centaurs—creatures human from the waist up and horses from the waist down.

Above: *This monstrous centaur, armed with a rock and an uprooted tree, decorated an ancient Greek vase.*

have originated somewhere around the Ural River, in what is now western Kazakhstan. During the eighth century BCE, they migrated westward to the region north of the Caucasus Mountains and the Black Sea. This was the territory of a people known as the Cimmerians, but the Scythians drove them out. Some Cimmerians moved into Asia Minor, while the Scythians pursued others across the Caucasus and into the Assyrian Empire based in Mesopotamia (modern Iraq).

Assyrian records referred to the Scythians as the Ishkuza or Ashkuzai, mentioning them for the first time in the late seventh century BCE. Led by a chief named Ishpakai, around 678 they allied with the Medes (from Media, a kingdom in what is now northern Iran) and waged war against the Assyrians. Only a few years later, though, a group of Scythians became allies of Assyria, and their chief, Bartatua, married an Assyrian princess. Bartatua's Scythians then proceeded to go after the Cimmerians in Asia Minor, who had been harassing Assyria's borders. Several decades later Bartatua's son, Madyes, came to the Assyrians' aid again, this time against the Medes. The Scythians took control of Media themselves and around 610 they and the Medes conquered Nineveh, the Assyrian Empire's capital.

Scythian warriors apparently raided many areas of the Middle East during this period, striking even as far south as Egypt. The biblical prophet Jeremiah expressed the settled people's horror at the nomads' attacks: "Behold, a people shall come from the north, and a great nation, and many kings shall be raised up from the coasts of the earth. They shall hold the bow and the lance: they are cruel, and will not show mercy: their voice shall roar like the sea, and they shall ride upon horses, every one put in array, like a man to battle, against thee." The fifth-century BCE Greek historian Herodotus wrote that for twenty-eight years the Scythians ruled west Asia "and the whole land was ruined because of their violence and their pride, for, besides exacting tribute . . . they rode about the land carrying off everyone's possessions."

After the conquest of Nineveh, however, the Medes rebelled, killed the Scythians' leaders, and drove the horsemen back north of the Caucasus. Herodotus tells us that "when the Scythians . . . returned to their country after so long an absence, as much trouble as their Median war awaited them. They found themselves opposed by a great force; for the Scythian women, when their husbands were away for so long, turned to their slaves." After much fighting, one of the returning warriors said to the others,

> "Men of Scythia, look at what we are doing! We are fighting our own slaves; they kill us, and we grow fewer; we kill them, and shall have fewer slaves. Now, then, my opinion is that we should drop our spears and bows, and meet them with horsewhips in our hands. As long as they see us armed, they imagine that they are our equals and the sons of our equals; let them see us with whips and no weapons, and they will perceive that they are our slaves; and taking this to heart they will not face our attack."

His advice worked: the slaves were shocked and shamed by being treated as animals instead of equals, and they fled rather than continue fighting.

We don't know how much of this story is true, but there was at least one thing that Herodotus misunderstood: he assumed that a Scythian with only a horsewhip was unarmed. In Scythian hands, however, the whip was a formidable weapon, used to strike at an enemy's face and eyes in close combat. Although the nomads' main weapons were bows and arrows, they had plenty of other options: lance or spear, axe, long sword, short sword or dagger, chain flail, and whip. They carried shields that might be plated with iron, which they often wore on their backs to keep their hands free and give them added protection from behind. High-ranking warriors had elaborate armor, made of overlapping metal scales sewn onto a leather jacket. Some also had helmets and leg coverings made in the same way. In battle, a Scythian warrior was prepared for anything.

THE SCYTHIANS' MAIN WEAPON WAS A SHORT COMPOSITE RECURVED BOW. *COMPOSITE* means that it was made of more than one material: a wooden core with sheets of bone or horn and other reinforcers glued on in layers. *Recurved* means that when the bow was unstrung, it curved in the opposite direction from when it was strung. The composite construction gave it extra strength, and the recurve gave it extra power. An arrow shot from such a bow could travel fifty yards a second and pierce metal armor. The Scythians carried their arrows and bows, ready for use at a moment's notice, in a case called a *gorytus* that hung from their belt. When they rode into battle, their favorite tactics included raining down arrows on their enemies from a distance and encircling them in order to give targets to as many archers as possible. Nomad archers shot with great accuracy and speed—as many as twenty arrows a minute. The onslaught was terrifying, and the aftermath could be horrible. Scythian arrowheads typically had three barbs, making them difficult to remove from wounds without causing greater injury. Moreover, according to many ancient sources, the Scythians and Sarmatians used poisoned arrows. The poison, called *scythicon* by Greek writers, was made from a mixture of snake venom, blood, and dung. If an enemy wasn't killed by his injury, *scythicon* would finish him off. As Ovid put it, "the flying metal" promised "a double death."

Above: *Unhorsed during battle, Scythian warriors stand back to back, their skill in archery still a threat to the enemy.*

PERSIAN PROBLEMS

THE SCYTHIANS AND SARMATIANS SPOKE LANGUAGES THAT were part of the Iranian language family. Another language that belonged to this family was Persian. But although Scythians and Persians were distantly related by language, their relationship was generally not a friendly one. When Cyrus the Great took over the old Assyrian and Median territory, establishing the first Persian empire, he found his northern borders constantly threatened by nomad horse archers, called Sakas in Persian.

Persian writers identified several different groups of Sakas, including the western ones known to the Greeks as Scythians. Other Sakas lived much farther to the east, pasturing their animals not only on the Central Asian steppe but in the high mountain meadows of the Tien Shan and Altai ranges, all the way on the edge of Siberia. Some modern scholars regard the Sakas of Central Asia as eastern Scythians. Others believe they were a "Scythian-type" people—similar to the

Opposite page: An envoy from the Sakas offers gold neck rings to the Persian ruler Darius I. This is part of a relief in Darius's palace that shows a procession of representatives from twenty-three subject peoples bringing tribute to their Persian overlord.

19

Scythians in their customs and language, but having enough cultural (and perhaps ethnic) differences to make them distinct.

POINTED-HAT SAKAS

Herodotus wrote that the wide plain east of the Caspian Sea was home to the Massagetae, who were

> like the Scythians in their dress and way of life. They are both cavalry and infantry (having some of each kind), and spearmen and archers; and it is their custom to carry battle-axes. They always use gold and bronze; all their spear-points and arrow-heads and battle-axes are bronze and the adornment of their headgear and belts . . . is gold. They equip their horses similarly, protecting their chests with bronze breastplates and putting gold on reins, bits, and cheekplates.

Herodotus did not think the Massagetae were Scythians, but many other ancient historians did. Modern scholars include the Massagetae among the Sakas, and some think they may have been a division of the people whom the Persians called Saka Tigrakhauda, or "pointed-hat Sakas." In any case, they were one of the nomad tribes living across Persia's borders, and Cyrus was determined to add their territory to his empire.

At that time, according to Herodotus, the Massagetae were ruled by a widowed queen, Tomyris. Cyrus sent her a message saying he wanted to marry her, but she refused, knowing that what he really wanted was her people's lands. Since he couldn't get them through marriage, he prepared to invade. Now Tomyris sent him a message: "Stop hurrying on what you are hurrying on, for you cannot know

Curled-up wild felines were among the designs often used for the gold plaques with which Sakas decorated their clothing and horse gear. This one comes from the region near the Altai Mountains, where many gold mines were located. The circular areas on the plaque probably held turquoise stones.

whether the completion of this work will be for your advantage. Stop, and be king of your own country; and endure seeing us ruling those whom we rule."

Cyrus did not stop. In the summer of 530 BCE he led his army into the nomads' territory. The Persians met with success early on, killing a large number of Massagetae warriors and capturing Tomyris's son. When Tomyris heard of this, she sent another message to Cyrus: "Do not be elated by what you have done. . . . Take a word of good advice from me: give me back my son and leave this country. . . . But if you will not, then I swear to you by the sun . . . that I shall give even you who can never get enough of it your fill of blood."

Cyrus ignored this threat, and Tomyris's son killed himself rather than endure captivity. Herodotus continues the story:

> Tomyris, when Cyrus would not listen to her, collected all her forces and engaged him. This fight I judge to have been the fiercest ever fought by men that were not Greek. . . . For first (it is said) they shot arrows at each other from a distance; then, when their arrows were all spent, they rushed at each other and fought with their spears and swords; and for a long time they stood fighting and neither would give ground; but at last the Massagetae got the upper hand. The greater part of the Persian army was destroyed there on the spot, and Cyrus

A fifteenth-century Italian painting of Tomyris, holding a spear and wearing armor under her gown. Thanks to Herodotus, the Massagetae queen was famous as one of the heroic women of history.

PERSIAN PROBLEMS 21

himself fell there. . . . Tomyris filled a skin with human blood, and searched among the Persian dead for Cyrus' body; and when she found it, she pushed his head into the skin, and insulted the dead man in these words: "Though I am alive and have defeated you in battle, you have destroyed me, taking my son by guile; but just as I threatened, I give you your fill of blood."

Cyrus was succeeded by Darius I, who continued to fight the steppe peoples, winning a great victory in 520 BCE. He had it recorded in an inscription: "I went to Saka land with an army against the Sakas who wear a pointed hat. When I arrived at the sea I went beyond it with all my army. Afterwards I severely defeated the Sakas. One [chief] I took captive, who was led bound to me and I slew him. Then I made another one chief, as was my wish. . . . Afterwards that land became mine."

A messenger brings news to Darius and his council as they make plans for war. This is part of a scene from a large wine jar painted by a fourth-century BCE Greek artist.

THE INVASION OF SCYTHIA

Darius was not finished with the nomads, or with building his empire. It already stretched from Asia Minor to what is now Pakistan, and he wanted to add Greece as well. First, however, he had to deal with the Scythians, who by this time held the north Black Sea region between the Danube and Don rivers. So, in about 513 BCE, Darius led a huge army up through Mesopotamia and Asia Minor to the Bosporus, the narrow strait at the western end of the Black Sea. Having crossed it, he moved into the eastern Balkan region known as Thrace, which he conquered. Then he continued north to the Danube, where he had a floating bridge built and marched his army over it and into Scythia.

Meanwhile, the Scythians had been preparing for the invasion of their lands. They had tried to enlist help from among the neighboring peoples, but only a few tribes joined with them. Their most important allies were the Sauromatians, Iranian-speaking nomads whose territory was the steppe between the Don and Volga rivers. There were three major groups of Scythians, and the Sauromatians were added to the one defending the area around the Don. The other two Scythian divisions, together with the additional allies they'd found, united under the leadership of the most powerful Scythian ruler, Idanthyrsus.

Then, according to Herodotus, "The Scythians sent an advance guard of their best horsemen to meet Darius' army. As for the wagons in which their children and wives lived, all these they sent forward, with instructions to drive always northward; and they sent all their flocks with the wagons, keeping none back except what was required for their food." The Scythian plan was to lead the Persians on an exhausting chase through a barren land, always staying a day's march ahead of the invaders. As the warriors passed through an area, they burned the pastures and clogged the springs and wells

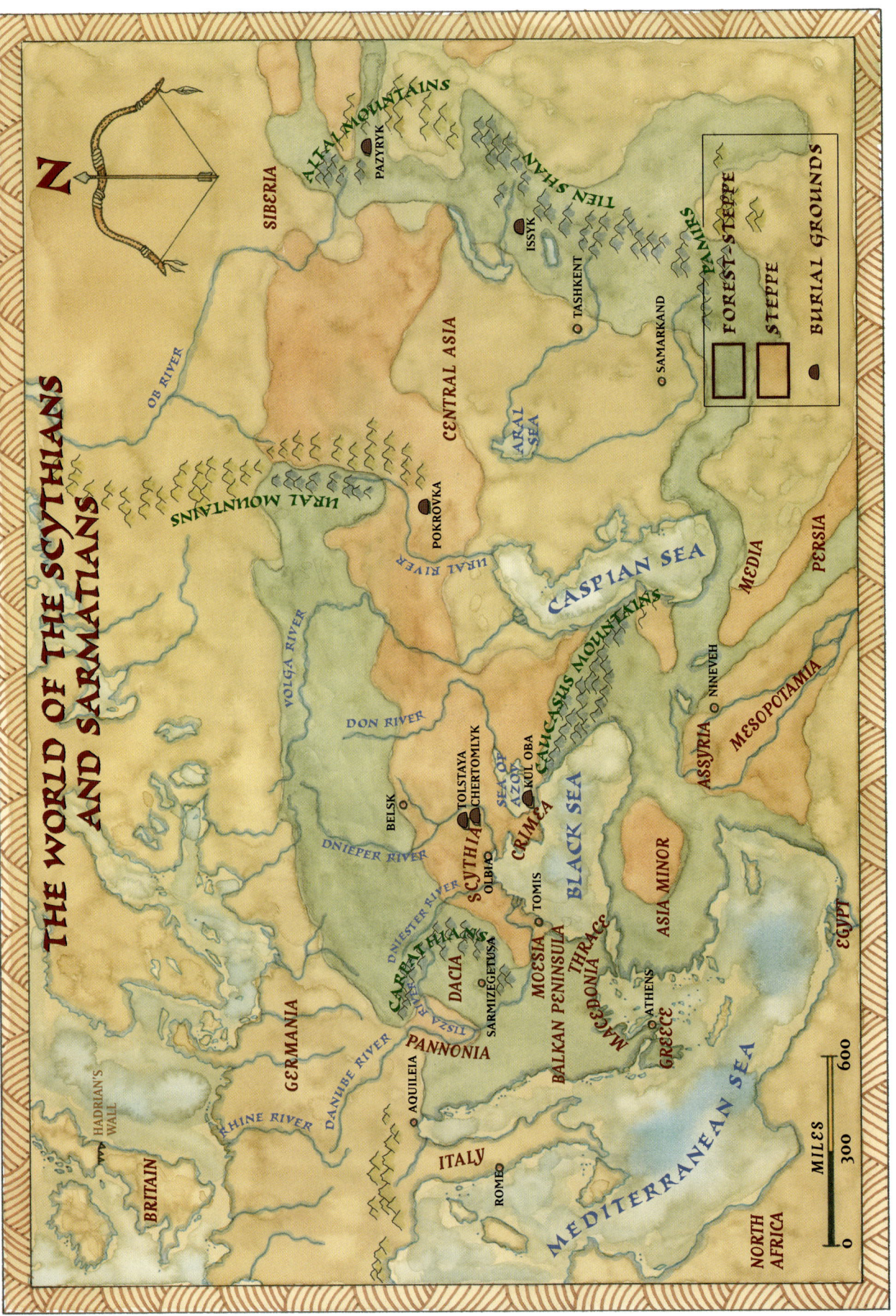

behind them so that the Persians would be deprived of water and other resources.

The Scythians' tactics succeeded in frustrating Darius and demoralizing his men. Herodotus tells us that after weeks of marching through Scythia without ever meeting the enemy, Darius sent a rider to Idanthyrsus with this message: "You crazy man, why do you always run, when you can do otherwise? If you believe yourself strong enough to withstand my power, stand and fight and stop running; but if you know you are the weaker, then stop running like this and come to terms with your master." Idanthyrsus answered, "Persian, such is my nature: I have never yet fled from any man in fear, nor am I fleeing now from you. . . . But you will yet weep bitter tears for having claimed to be my master."

Idanthyrsus now summoned the Scythians and Sauromatians who had been stationed at the Don, ordering them to harass Persian scouting parties by day and attack Persian encampments by night. After a number of these attacks, the Scythian leaders sent Darius a bird, a mouse, a frog, and five arrows. "The Persians asked the bearer of these gifts what they meant; but he . . . told the Persians to figure out what the presents meant themselves, if they were smart enough." Darius decided the gifts must symbolize the Scythians' surrender, but a man named Gobryas had a different interpretation: "Unless you become birds, Persians, and fly up into the sky, or mice and hide in the earth, or frogs and leap into the lakes, you will be shot by these arrows and never return home."

Herodotus continues the story:

> After sending the gifts to Darius, the Scythians who had remained there came out with foot and horse and offered battle to the Persians. But when the Scythian ranks were set in order, a rabbit ran out between the armies; and every Scythian

that saw it gave chase. So there was confusion and shouting among the Scythians; Darius asked about the clamor among the enemy; and when he heard that they were chasing a rabbit, he said to those with whom he was accustomed to speak, "These men hold us in deep contempt; and I think now that Gobryas' opinion of the Scythian gifts was true."

That very night, leaving behind the sick and wounded, Darius and the rest of his army snuck away back to the Danube and from there returned to Persian territory. The Scythians had beaten one of the world's mightiest empires without ever fighting a battle.

SCYTHIAN RELIGION

WHEN DARIUS DEMANDED THE SCYTHIANS' SURRENDER AND CLAIMED TO BE THEIR master, part of Idanthyrsus's reply was, "As to masters, I acknowledge Zeus my forefather and Hestia queen of the Scythians only." Herodotus reported this using Greek names, but elsewhere in his history he gave the native names of the Scythian goddesses and gods as well as the Greek deities he thought they most resembled. First among them was Tabiti, compared to Hestia, goddess of the hearth. Next were Papaeus and his wife Apia, whom Herodotus likened to Zeus (father god and god of the sky and storms) and Earth. Then came Goetosyrus and Argimpasa, identified by Herodotus with Apollo (god of the sun, the arts, and healing) and Heavenly Aphrodite (goddess of love). There were also a god of strength and a god of war (Heracles and Ares in Greek; Herodotus apparently did not learn their Scythian names). All of these deities were worshipped by all Scythians, according to Herodotus. In addition, one group of Scythians honored Thagimasadas, whom Herodotus interpreted as Poseidon, god of the sea, earthquakes, and—most importantly to the Scythians—horses. But the only deity the Scythians made images or altars for was the war god.

Horses had great spiritual meaning, especially at death and in the afterlife. This mask made of gold, leather, felt, and fur was worn by one of ten horses buried with a chief at Pazyryk in the Altai Mountains. The mask is crowned by a fantastic animal with horns and wings, perhaps a symbol of transformation.

LIFE and DEATH on the STEPPE

CONSIDERING DARIUS'S INVASION OF SCYTHIA, HERODOTUS concluded,

> Though in most respects I do not admire them, [the Scythians] have managed one thing . . . better than anyone else on the face of the earth: I mean their own preservation. For such is their manner of life that no one who invades their country can escape destruction, and if they wish to avoid engaging with an enemy, that enemy cannot by any possibility come to grips with them. A people without fortified towns, living as the Scythians do, in wagons which they take with them wherever they go, accustomed . . . to fight on horseback with bows and arrows, and dependent for their food not upon agriculture but upon their cattle: how can such a people fail to defeat the attempt of an invader not only to subdue them, but even to make contact with them?

Opposite page: In a ceremony of brotherhood, two Scythian men drink together from the same drinking horn. This two-inch-high gold plaque was one of the treasures found in the Kul Oba burial mound in the Crimea.

No wonder Darius was forced to give up on conquering the Scythians. He was still determined to take over Greece, however, and his successor, Xerxes, continued this effort. From 499 to 448 BCE a series of wars raged between the Greeks and Persians. These wars were the main subject of Herodotus's history, but he also investigated many related matters, which was how he came to write about the Scythians. We are lucky he did so, because his work is one of our most important sources of information about life among these nomad archers.

HERODOTUS INVESTIGATES

Originally from a Greek colony in Asia Minor, Herodotus traveled a great deal to do research for his writings. Wherever he went, he talked to the local people and learned about their customs, legends, and history. Around the year 450 BCE he visited Olbia, a Greek colony on the north coast of the Black Sea. Olbia was a major center for trade and communication between Greeks and Scythians. One of the people Herodotus met there was the Scythian king's official representative in the town. Herodotus also seems to have traveled at least a little way north onto the steppe, and he seems to have enjoyed seeing the Dnieper River and the countryside around it.

By Herodotus's time, Scythian culture was undergoing changes, partly because of increased contact with the Greeks. Many Scythians had settled down to farm, and they exported huge amounts of grain to Greece. Scythians also supplied the Greeks with slaves, livestock, and

Herodotus, known as the Father of History. Even our word *history* comes from Herodotus, who titled his book *Historiai,* an ancient Greek term that meant "questions," "inquiries," or "researches."

animal products such as furs and leather. Elite Scythians were beginning to enjoy Greek luxuries, especially wine, and to employ Greek craftspeople to make gold and silver jewelry and other objects. The artisans worked to order, producing the same sorts of things as Scythian metalworkers did, featuring ornate and fantastical images of animals. The Greeks also made lively lifelike portrayals of the Scythians themselves to decorate a variety of items, such as combs, neck rings, cups, and vases.

Herodotus's written portrait of the Scythians was equally lively. For instance, he described how the Scythians made vows of loyalty:

> As for giving sworn pledges to those who are to receive them, . . . they take blood from the parties to the agreement by making a little cut in the body with an awl or a knife, and pour it mixed with wine into a big earthenware bowl, into which they then dip a [sword] and arrows and an axe and a [spear]; and when this is done those swearing the agreement, and the most honorable of their followers, drink the blood.

This realistic image of a Scythian warrior assisting his friend with a toothache or mouth injury was made by a Greek craftsman. The scene comes from a five-inch-high vase made from a blend of gold and silver, found in the Kul Oba burial mound. Other scenes on the vase show warriors talking together, stringing a bow, and bandaging a leg wound.

This procedure was also followed when two men declared themselves blood brothers, bound to support and defend each other to the death. They sealed their oath by drinking the mixed blood and wine from the same cup at the same time.

When people wanted to make the mightiest vow possible, they swore by the king's hearth. If someone broke such a vow, the Scythians believed the king would become ill. So when a king got sick, it was important to find out who had made a false oath. Discovering the culprit was the job of diviners called Enarees. These men said that a goddess "gave them the art of divination, which they practise by means of lime-tree [linden] bark. They cut this bark into three portions, and prophesy while they braid and unbraid these in their fingers."

Diviners also used willow wands: "They bring great bundles of wands, which they lay on the ground and unfasten, and utter their divinations as they lay the rods down one by one; and while still speaking, they gather up the rods once more and place them together again." Prophecy and divination were well known in the Greek world, although the Scythians' methods would have seemed exotically different. Many of Herodotus's readers may have been shocked by the Enarees themselves, men who wore women's clothing and lived as women in most other respects.

Scythian customs related to warfare, too, probably seemed shockingly barbaric:

> A Scythian drinks the blood of the first man whom he has taken down. He carries the heads of all whom he has slain in the battle to his king; for if he brings a head, he receives a share of the booty taken, but not otherwise. He scalps the head. . . . He keeps [the scalp] for a hand towel, fastening it to the bridle of [his] horse . . . and taking pride in it; for he who has most scalps . . . is judged the best man. . . . The heads themselves, not all of them but those of their bitterest enemies, they treat this way. Each saws off all the part beneath the eyebrows, and cleans the rest. If he is a poor man, then he covers the outside with a piece of raw hide, and so makes use of it; but if he is rich, he covers the [skull] with the raw hide, and gilds the inside of it and uses it for a drinking-cup.

Archaeologists have found evidence to support Herodotus's story at a site now known as Belsk, on a tributary of the Dnieper River. Within the fortifications of this sprawling settlement were three villages, a cemetery, areas for livestock to graze, grain warehouses, and a variety of craft workshops. The people of Belsk made pottery, horse gear, leather goods, jewelry, bronze arrowheads, and a variety of iron objects. In one very specialized workshop, craftspeople turned the tops of human skulls into drinking cups.

To many readers, in both ancient and more recent times, Herodotus's description of a Scythian royal funeral seemed even more incredible than his story of Scythian head collecting. He wrote, "They take the king's corpse and, having opened the belly and cleaned out the inside, fill it with a preparation of chopped cypress, frankincense, parsley seed, and aniseed, after which they sew up the opening, enclose the body in wax and, placing it on a wagon, carry it through all the different tribes." This funeral procession through the dead king's lands took forty days, then arrived at the traditional burial site for Scythian rulers.

A bronze pin depicts a Scythian warrior displaying the head of an enemy—or perhaps of a relative. Herodotus wrote that sometimes a Scythian man made a skull cup "out of the head of his own kinsman with whom he has been feuding, and whom he has defeated in single combat before the king."

> There the body of the dead king is laid in the grave prepared for it, stretched upon a mattress. . . . In the open space around the king they bury one of his [wives or servant girls], first killing her by strangling, and also his cupbearer, his cook, his groom, his lackey, his messenger, his horses, firstlings of all his other possessions and some golden cups. . . . After this they set to work and raise a vast mound above the grave, all of them vying with each other and seeking to make it as tall as possible.

The final ceremonies came a year later, when "they take the most trusted of the rest of the king's servants . . . and strangle fifty of these and fifty of their best horses and empty and clean the bellies of them all, fill them with chaff, and sew them up again." Then they set the dead men on the dead horses, arranged upright in a circle around the mound, looking just as if the late king's servants had mounted guard on his grave.

TESTIMONY OF THE TOMBS

Archaeological finds have shown there was much truth in Herodotus's description of Scythian funeral ceremonies. Until the modern age, the steppe was dotted with thousands of kurgans, or burial mounds. Often three stories high (or more) and clustered together in large groups, these kurgans could be seen across the flat steppe from miles away. Most of them were robbed in earlier times, and a great many have eroded and been plowed over. Nevertheless, a number of surviving mounds have yielded amazing discoveries.

A partly eroded kurgan in south-eastern Kazakhstan, where the steppe gives way to the foothills of the Tien Shan

In a sixth-century BCE kurgan in the northern Caucasus, a Russian archaeologist found the remains of 360 horses carefully arranged around wooden pillars in the burial chamber. A third of the way up the mound, in a layer probably constructed at some point after the funeral (perhaps a year later, as Herodotus wrote), there were so many horses that the archaeologist gave up on counting them. In another Caucasus kurgan, twenty-nine horse skeletons lay in a circle around the burial chamber, while still another had thirteen horses lined up neatly beside and at the foot of the dead person.

The largest of all Scythian kurgans dates to the fourth century BCE. Sixty feet high and more than a thousand feet around at the base, it was excavated in 1862 at Chertomlyk in today's Ukraine. In a great stroke of luck, the archaeologists found this tomb had been only partially robbed. Most of the tomb's amazing treasures were still in place: thousands of gold ornaments, hundreds of bronze arrowheads, swords and spears, bronze cauldrons, gold and silver cups, and more.

Inside the mound were several burial chambers, the main one for a king or powerful chief. Three other chambers held the skeletons of four male guards or servants. In another chamber lay a woman. She was wearing a gold neck ring and gold earrings, bracelets, and rings—one on each finger. She had been dressed in a purple garment, but little of the cloth remained, although its decorations were there: fifty-seven square plaques of gold. Near her coffin was a splendid

Fourteen horse skeletons were found in this kurgan in the Altai Mountains in 2001. The burial mound also revealed the remains of a man and woman whose clothes were covered with thousands of small, gold, leopard-shaped plaques.

LIFE AND DEATH ON THE STEPPE

amphora, or Greek wine jar. More than two feet tall, it was made of silver and gold and decorated with depictions of real and mythological animals as well as scenes of Scythian men training horses. The lady's dead cupbearer lay in the chamber, too. The Chertomlyk mound also contained three pits that held the skeletons of eleven horses, together with two grooms to care for them in the afterlife.

Another Ukrainian tomb, known as the Tolstaya mound, was carefully excavated in 1971. The archaeologists estimated that 1,300 people took part in its construction and in the feast after the funeral. The remains of pottery amphoras showed that the people drank to the dead with huge quantities of Greek wine. The animal bones found on the site showed they ate even more than they drank—a total of some 14,000 pounds of meat, including at least 14 wild boars.

Modern scholars believe Tolstaya and other kurgans were built by members of the tribe who volunteered for this duty. They used pieces of turf, each about six inches thick, to construct a kind of earthen pyramid. The grassy sod probably symbolized a heavenly pasture where the dead continued to exist in the same way they had during life, riding their horses and grazing their livestock in the endless grasslands.

THE REAL AMAZONS

The tombs revealed something else. More than forty of the kurgans explored by archaeologists in Scythian territory contained the graves of women warriors. The oldest of these dates to the fourth century BCE. The dead woman was buried not only with jewelry, pottery, a bronze mirror, and a spindle (a tool for spinning wool into thread), but also two long iron spear points and a quiver filled with forty-seven arrows. At her feet lay the skeleton of a young man, who took only an iron ring and two small bells into the afterlife with him. A woman in another kurgan had similar grave goods and weapons, as well as a belt reinforced with iron strips (a common piece of Scythian armor). Other Scythian women

LIFE AND DEATH IN PAZYRYK

SOME OF THE MOST SPECTACULAR DISCOVERIES OF STEPPE NOMAD TOMBS OCCURRED in the Altai Mountains' Pazyryk valley in the late 1940s. Permafrost in these kurgans preserved materials, such as cloth and wood, that decomposed in other conditions. Even some of the bodies were found nearly intact, revealing that they had been cleaned out and stuffed with herbs and other plants, much as Herodotus described when he wrote of Scythian death customs. A warrior-chief buried in the fourth century was so well preserved that his tattoos were still vivid: a fish on his right shin, deer and a mountain goat on his left arm, a winged monster and an eagle-beaked deer on his right arm, a griffin twining from his chest around to his back, and many more.

Numerous horses were found in the Pazyryk tombs, too, with saddles and bridles still in place. One kurgan had ten fine reddish-furred horses wearing colorful felt saddlecloths decorated with images of real and fantastic creatures. Two of the horses wore masks that made them look like fantastic creatures themselves, with feathers, horns, and antlers made of felt or leather. Their bridles were decorated with gilded wooden carvings of animals.

The Pazyryk tombs contained many other rare objects that have given us a better idea of how ancient steppe nomads lived. In addition to bows, arrows, and other weapons, there were easy-to-transport collapsible tables; clay jars and cups; hangings, mats, and rugs of wool and felt; and musical instruments, including harps and tambourines. Clothing, colorfully decorated, was made from wool, hemp, fur, and leather; the archaeologists found jackets, tunics, hoods and caps, felt stockings, boots, and even baby clothes. One woman had leopard-skin boots with beaded designs on the bottoms. Other items buried with the Pazyryk dead showed that these nomads engaged in wide-ranging trade: the grave goods included cheetah fur from the Middle East, carpets from Persia, and silk and mirrors from China.

Above: *This Pazyryk chieftain's grave goods included a finely woven carpet, about six feet square, with multicolored images of horses and riders marching from left to right around the edge. Various features of its design have led archaeologists to theorize that the carpet was used not just as a ground covering or wall hanging but also as a game board.*

An Amazon appears to be already taking aim at her target even as she reaches into her quiver for an arrow. This bronze figure, a decoration on the rim of a bowl, was made in Italy around 480 BCE—Amazons had become popular subjects of artwork and stories among the Greeks and other Mediterranean peoples.

buried with weapons had obvious battle injuries, such as an arrowhead stuck in the knee. Modern archaeologists have no doubt that these women were trained and experienced fighters.

German archaeologist Renate Rolle found women warriors in six out of the fifty-three kurgans she investigated at Chertomlyk in the 1980s. She described a burial that particularly moved her: "One was a young woman with weapons, a bow and some arrowheads, and this little child lying on her arm. The two fingers of her right hand which would have had heavy use from pulling a bow showed clear signs of wear and tear." Rolle theorized that Scythian warrior women "may have led perfectly normal married lives together with their family and husbands. They only fought when they had to, to defend their settlement, or if there was some particularly ferocious fighting going on."

The first-century BCE historian Diodorus Siculus told of a time when "there came in Scythia a period of revolutions, in which the sovereigns were women endowed with exceptional valour. For among these peoples the women train for war just as do the men. . . . Consequently distinguished women have been the authors of many great deeds, not in Scythia alone, but also in the territory bordering upon it." The territory east of the Scythians was home to the Sauromatians (or Sauromatae), another group of steppe nomads. Out of all the excavated

Sauromatian warrior burials from the fifth and fourth centuries BCE, 20 percent belonged to women.

Until the late twentieth century, most scholars thought warrior women like these were just figures of legend. With some exceptions like Diodorus, few people believed what Herodotus had written: "The women of the Sauromatae . . . ride out hunting, with their men or without them; they go to war, and dress the same as the men. . . . In regard to marriage, it is the custom that no maiden weds until she has killed a man of the enemy; and some of them grow old and die unmarried, because they cannot fulfill the law." Another Greek writer of the same period added, "A woman who takes to herself a husband no longer rides, unless she is compelled to do so by a general expedition."

According to Herodotus, the Sauromatian people had their beginnings in marriages between a group of Scythian men and a group of Amazons, warrior women originally from Asia Minor. This part of the story may well be legend, but archaeology has certainly shown that fighting women, many of them in their teens and twenties, were an important part of Sauromatian society. They may have been even more important among a people with a similar name, the Sarmatians. Like the Scythians and Sauromatians, the Sarmatians were steppe nomads who spoke an Iranian language. The Sarmatians originally lived east of the Sauromatians, and their population probably included people from the forest-steppes. Some ancient writers gave the Sarmatians a Greek nickname that meant "women-ruled."

The earliest archaeological evidence of the Sarmatians' culture was found in kurgans along the Ural River.* In the 1990s American archaeologist Jeannine Davis-Kimball excavated a number of these

A bone spindle from the fourth century BCE, found in a kurgan in the region northwest of the Sea of Azov

*This area was also home to Sauromatians before they were displaced or absorbed by the Sarmatians. Archaeologists are able to tell which group the kurgans belonged to because the Sauromatians buried their dead with the head pointing to the east, while in Sarmatian burials the head pointed to the south.

LIFE AND DEATH ON THE STEPPE

at a site called Pokrovka in the southern Ural Mountains. This was not a royal cemetery, but one for ordinary people. The vast majority of the men—94 percent—were buried with weapons, while 3 percent had only a clay pot to take with them to the otherworld. Another 3 percent were buried with few grave goods and a child at their side, for reasons that are still not clear. This surprised archaeologists especially because they didn't find any children in the Sarmatian women's graves.

The women at Pokrovka were buried with a much wider, and richer, array of items, including spindles, gilded bronze spiral earrings, bronze mirrors, and clothing trimmed with hundreds of imported tiny jet beads. They also had bead jewelry made from glass, amber, turquoise, carnelian, and other stones—all materials that came from faraway lands. In this early Sarmatian cemetery, 15 percent of the women were warriors, buried with arrowheads and other weapons. Sometimes they had amulets to give them added strength—one woman, for example, wore a boar's tusk hanging from a cord around her waist. Other grave goods showed that some of these warriors also served as priestesses. Moreover, in 72 percent of the Pokrovka kurgans, the central grave—the position of highest status—belonged to a woman. Davis-Kimball believes the evidence all adds up to show that among these steppe nomads, women had wealth, power, and leading positions in family and tribe.

WOMEN OF SPIRIT

IN HER STUDIES OF POKROVKA AND OTHER NOMAD SITES, JEANNINE DAVIS-KIMBALL discovered sets of distinctive objects that showed their users were priestesses. These items included small portable altars, carved bone spoons, bronze mirrors, and amulets in the shape of animals. Sometimes chunks of colored minerals were found, too, which could be ground into powders. Many archaeologists have believed such powders were used as cosmetics, but Davis-Kimball thinks the priestesses used them to draw symbolic designs on their bodies. The mirrors, too, were probably for symbolic, religious purposes, used in divination and healing. These were among the priestesses' main duties, along with making regular offerings—of milk, koumiss, cheese, and meat—to the gods and other spirits.

Some priestesses were also warriors, but earlier archaeologists often didn't recognize the fact. A discovery made in a Saka kurgan at Issyk in 1969 revealed the skeleton of a small-boned person a little over five feet tall, buried in the fifth century BCE. The body was covered with four thousand golden plaques, originally sewn to clothing and boots. The discoverer named the dead person, who was buried with weapons, the Issyk Gold Man. But in the 1990s Davis-Kimball noticed that the burial contained items not found with early nomad men, such as gold and turquoise earrings, equipment for making koumiss, and a mirror. Considering these objects, the person's small size, and other factors, Davis-Kimball concluded that the Gold Man was really a Gold Woman, and a warrior-priestess of high rank and importance.

Above: *This Greek-crafted golden image of a Scythian goddess—probably Tabiti—was made to be worn as a pendant. It is actually no bigger than a thimble.*

PEOPLES on the MOVE

ARCHAEOLOGISTS THINK THAT DURING THE SIXTH CENTURY BCE, Scythians and Sauromatians mingled more or less peacefully in the region north of the Caucasus. Gradually, however, conflict between the two peoples increased. The Sauromatians pushed west with greater and greater force, till by Herodotus's time the Scythians had lost their lands east of the Don River. The Scythians continued to thrive north of the Black Sea, however, growing rich from their trade with the Greeks. For a time they enjoyed a golden age of power and prosperity. But new forces stirring both west and east would soon bring new challenges to the Scythians.

SCYTHIAN LAST STANDS

The king who reigned over Scythia during its golden age in the fourth century BCE was Ateas. It was said that he had united all the Scythian peoples between the Danube and the Don under his sole rule. Then he expanded the Scythian realm west, capturing territory on the other side

Opposite page: A Greek artist worked amazing detail into this two-inch-long plaque, from the fourth-century BCE Kul Oba burial. The designs on the rider's clothing may be meant to indicate gold plaques (like this one) sewn onto the jacket and trousers.

of the Danube, in what is now Romania. As he pushed south into the Balkan Peninsula, however, he soon came to the attention of another king who was expanding his realm, Philip II of Macedonia.

Philip sent ambassadors to Ateas. When they went before the Scythian king, he was grooming his horse, which he continued to do as the ambassadors made their presentation. Apparently, Ateas responded simply by asking if Philip groomed his own horse, too. It may have been during this embassy, or another one, that Philip sent a message stating his desire to be named Ateas's heir. Ateas answered, scornfully, that he already had a son and heir.

Next Philip announced he was going to set up a bronze statue of Hercules at the Danube's mouth. Ateas knew this was just Philip's excuse to enter Scythian lands, so he said Philip should send him the statue and he would see to setting it up himself. But if Philip went ahead and attempted to bring the statue into Scythia without Ateas's permission, then Ateas swore his warriors would destroy it and make arrowheads from the bronze.

On a gold coin issued during his reign, Philip II is portrayed wearing the laurel wreath of the Greek god Apollo.

This was apparently one challenge too many for Philip. In 339 BCE he marched his army against the Scythians. Ateas, although he was reported to be ninety years old at the time, personally led his warriors into battle. The details of the encounter have not come down to us, but the result has. Ateas was killed in the fighting, and the Macedonians captured and enslaved thousands of Scythian women and children. They also acquired Scythian livestock, including, it was said, 20,000 horses. Philip's victory apparently loosened the Scythians' hold on their western lands, since the Getans began to settle between the

Danube and the Dnieper in large numbers. On the whole, however, the Scythian kingdom did not seem much weakened.

Philip was seriously wounded in the battle with Ateas, but he lived for three more years. He was succeeded by his son, Alexander the Great, who set out to conquer the world. In 331 BCE, while Alexander was fighting in Persia, one of his generals led an invasion of Scythia. He besieged Olbia, but not for long—the Scythian military was still a force to be reckoned with. The Scythians drove out the Macedonian army, inflicting one of the worst defeats of Alexander's career.

In 329 BCE Alexander himself, after subduing most of the Persian Empire, marched his army into the Central Asian lands southeast of the Aral Sea. This region was home to cities such as Samarkand and Tashkent, important stations along the main trade route between China and the Mediterranean. The people of these cities fiercely resisted Alexander and were helped by powerful allies, Sakas from the nearby steppes. In the spring of 328 BCE, however, the Sakas decided to make peace with Alexander.

Neither history nor legend has much to tell us about the Scythians or Sakas for some time after this. Scholars believe, however, that the Scythians were coming under increasing pressure from Celts and Getans to the west and Sarmatians to the east. By around 200 BCE the center of Scythian power had shifted to the Crimea, a peninsula jutting south into the Black Sea. Scythians had been living there for centuries, mingling with Greek colonists and often fighting as mercenaries in their wars. Now much of the Crimea became an independent Scythian kingdom, strong enough to demand tribute from its Greek neighbors.

The Crimean Scythians also raided a number of Greek cities around the Black Sea. The citizens eventually appealed for help to Mithradates the Great, ruler of a powerful kingdom in northern Asia Minor. Although the Scythians had help from a Sarmatian tribe, the Roxolani, Mithradates' forces defeated them in 106 BCE. Peace was made, and the

Mithradates the Great wearing the lion skin of Hercules, a symbol of strength and victory

Scythians became allies of Mithradates. To cement the relationship, Mithradates "gave his daughter in marriage to the Scythian rulers," according to one ancient historian. According to another, Mithradates in turn married several Scythian women, probably members of the royal family. Mithradates also incorporated Scythian warriors into his army.

After Mithradates died in 63 BCE, the Scythian kingdom entered a tumultuous time. The Scythian population blended with other peoples of the Crimea, including Sarmatians who had begun moving into the peninsula in the second century BCE. As the Roman Empire gained more control around the Black Sea, the Scythians were often caught up in the power struggles that resulted. Trade with the Greeks carried on in times of peace, however, so the kingdom remained fairly prosperous and stable. Only with the invasions of the Goths in the third century CE and the Huns in the fourth century did the Scythian kingdom finally crumble.

KNIGHTS IN ARMOR

The 300s BCE were a time of upheaval among the steppe nomads. It was during this century that the Sarmatians migrated into Sauromatian lands between the Volga and the Don. They absorbed some of the Sauromatian population, while other Sauromatians moved into Scythian territory. But the Sarmatians did not stop pushing westward. Some groups—raiding parties at the very least—struck deep into Scythia in the third century BCE. By 200 BCE or so, large numbers of

ANACHARSIS, POSSIBLY THE BROTHER OF A SCYTHIAN KING, WAS A RENOWNED WISE man. Around 590 BCE he visited Athens, Greece, the city regarded as the birthplace of philosophy. There he impressed the people so much that he became known as one of the fabled Seven Sages. At one point he was invited to a gathering of philosophers by Croesus, ruler of the kingdom of Lydia in Asia Minor. According to Diodorus Siculus, writing in the first century BCE, Croesus asked Anacharsis to name the bravest being on earth.

SCYTHIAN WISDOM

Anacharsis said: the wildest animals, for they alone died willingly for their freedom. Croesus thought that this was the wrong answer but believed that the answer to his second question would be according to his wish, and so he asked him whom he considered to be the most righteous. But Anacharsis answered again: the wildest animals, for they alone lived according to nature and not according to laws; and whereas nature was the work of God, the law was only the invention of man, and surely it was more just to abide by the works of God than by those of man. And now, wishing to get the better of Anacharsis, Croesus asked him whether he thought the wildest animals also the wisest: but [Anacharsis] declared this at once to be true, explaining that it was indeed a mark of wisdom to set the truth of nature above the statutes of the law. Croesus however ridiculed him, as if these answers savoured of Scythia and a [savage] way of life.

Above: A gold belt buckle from Saka lands depicts a fight between a tiger and a fantastic creature whose mane curls into birds' heads.

Sarmatians had migrated into the steppe north of the Black Sea, where they became the ruling elite. Diodorus Siculus gave a brief but dramatic summary of these events: "This people became powerful and ravaged a large part of Scythia, and destroying utterly all whom they subdued they turned most of the land into a desert."

In spite of this sweeping statement, the Sarmatians didn't leave the Black Sea steppe totally deserted. Perhaps the Scythian ruling class was driven out, but there must have been farmers and others left in the settled communities. Certainly the Sarmatians had no intention of taking up agriculture themselves. Rather, according to the Greek geographer Strabo, "They turn over their land to anyone who wishes to till it, requiring only that in return they receive the rent they have put on it." The Sarmatians focused their own efforts on herding, raiding, and war.

Like the Scythians and other steppe nomads, the Sarmatians were masters of mounted archery. In addition, they had developed their own unique methods of fighting. From horseback they wielded long swords to slash at their enemies. (Such swords have been found in the graves of women as well as men.) Many Sarmatian warriors were also armed with heavy lances. In battle they galloped in formation toward their enemies, leveling their lances directly at them. Before the Sarmatians, this kind of cavalry charge was rare in the ancient world. As the Roman historian Tacitus remarked, "The line of battle which can stand up to them hardly exists."

When the Sarmatian cavalry broke up an enemy line, the lancers were protected from counterattack by conical iron helmets, long-sleeved coats of armor, and armored trousers. Their horses, too, wore armor that protected their heads and bodies. Sarmatian armor was usually made of iron or bronze scales riveted onto leather or heavy cloth. Sometimes, though, the scales were made out of horn. Still another type of scale armor was described by the ancient historian Pausanias:

With men and horses alike protected by scale armor, Sarmatian warriors charge into battle. When this sculpture was first carved in second-century Rome, they would have been holding long lances in their hands, but this detail has not survived.

[The Sarmatians] collect the hoofs of their mares, clean them, and split them till they resemble the scales of a dragon. Anybody who has not seen a dragon has at least seen a green fir cone. Well, the fabric which they make out of the hoofs [is similar] to the clefts on a fir cone. In these pieces [of hoof] they bore holes, and having stitched them together with the sinews of horses and oxen, they use them as corselets [chest armor], which are . . . both sword-proof and arrow-proof.

By the first century BCE, there were several tribes of Sarmatians. East of the Don River were the Aorsi and Siraki. The territory between the

Don and the Dnieper was held by the Roxolani. Across the Dnieper were the Iazyges. The Sarmatians did not stay in these positions for long, however. As the first century BCE went on, each group kept pushing to the west. While the Siraki remained mainly in the Caucasus region, the Aorsi moved into the Crimea and the area around the Sea of Azov. The Roxolani shifted their center of power to the steppes west of the Dnieper. The Iazyges, in turn, were pushed to the Dniester River.

This pattern of migration continued over the next century or two—sometimes slowing down, sometimes speeding up—as one tribe pressured another in the search for new pastures. The problem was that the steppe did not extend westward forever. And at the point where the steppe ended, the Sarmatians found themselves running into the greatest of all barriers to their progress: the Roman Empire.

The Iazyges had their first run-in with Rome during the expanding empire's wars with Mithradates the Great in the 80s BCE. Fighting as allies of Mithradates, one of Rome's greatest enemies, the Iazyges made themselves targets of Roman revenge. In 78 BCE Roman troops crossed the Danube and campaigned in Iazyges territory for two years. They intended to teach these troublesome new barbarians a lesson and show them that Rome, not Mithradates, was the superpower of the region.

Later in the century, however, the superpower decided it could use the barbarians' help. North of the lower Danube, in what is now Romania, was the wealthy and powerful kingdom of Dacia, whose people seem to have been a mixture of Getans, Celts, and other ethnic groups. When Dacia began to show signs of falling apart, the Romans tried to weaken it further by allowing the Iazyges to move into the region. By the first decade BCE, the Iazyges seem to have been establishing themselves on the steppe to Dacia's east, between the

Carpathian Mountains and the Danube delta. The Roxolani then began to move into the Iazyges' old pastures. And some Sarmatians evidently became part of the Dacian kingdom. Although we don't know much about Dacia's history, we do know that the name of the capital city was Sarmizegetusa, which meant something like "the place of Sarmatians and Getans."

Soon the Romans must have begun to regret having Sarmatians living just across the Danube. In 6 CE a group of Iazyges and Dacians crossed the river to raid the Roman province of Moesia (today's northern Bulgaria). During Ovid's exile in Tomis, beginning in 9 CE, Sarmatian raids were frequent. The towns south of the Danube were particularly vulnerable in the winter, a season of hardship on the steppe. Ovid wrote:

> While summer lasts the Danube is our friend:
> His war-preventing water between us
> And them. But when the spiteful season shows
> His sordid face and grim frost grips the ground,
> Then are those savage peoples by the quaking cold
> Driven toward the limit of endurance.

In winters when the Danube froze over, the danger to the people around Tomis was even greater:

> When Danube by the north wind has been frozen flat:
> Then comes the enemy, riding to attack,
> Savaging the surroundings far and wide.

There was almost no way for people in the countryside to protect themselves from the raiders:

Ovid's terrifying description of barbarians on the attack comes alive in the imagination of a nineteenth-century French artist.

> Some flee, abandoning to plunder what little
> The country and the wretched peasant has.
> Others, dragged off with pinioned arms,
> Gaze helplessly behind toward families and farms.
> Yet others, shot with barbed shaft, fall writhing:
> For poison rides aboard the flying steel.

As soon as a Sarmatian raiding party was sighted, Ovid wrote, a general alarm went up. Every able-bodied man armed himself and manned the city walls—including the poet himself, who was in his fifties and had never wielded a sword in his life. He described seeing farmers and villagers running for the shelter of the city but unable to reach the gate before they were caught or killed by the raiders. Even those who'd made it in still feared for their safety:

> Now are the frighted walls made dizzy by the mounted archer
> As stockaded sheep are giddied by the circling wolf.
> Now is the shortbow, strung with horse hair, never slack.
> Our housetops bristle with a feathered mist of arrows
> And the stoutly crossbarred gate scarce counters the attack.

Luckily for Ovid and the rest, the Sarmatians never did manage to break into Tomis. Their style of warfare was not really suited to besieging cities or battering down walls. But their hit-and-run attacks and heavy cavalry charges were more than enough to make them formidable enemies—or, in the right circumstances, awesome allies.

ENEMIES and ALLIES

Not long after Sarmatians moved north of the Black Sea and into the Crimea, they involved themselves in conflicts among the Greek cities of the region. Sometimes they took one side, sometimes another. In 49 CE they became embroiled in a civil war in a Greek kingdom on the south shores of the Sea of Azov. The king, Mithradates (a descendant of Mithradates the Great), had been driven out by his younger brother, Cotys. Rome sided with Cotys and sent troops to support him. Then Cotys and the Roman commander learned the Siraki were going to fight for Mithradates.

Deciding they, too, needed Sarmatian allies, they contacted the king of the Aorsi. He was happy to enter into the alliance—since the Romans were more powerful than Mithradates, that was the side he wanted to be on. With the help of the Aorsi cavalry, Cotys and the Romans thoroughly defeated Mithradates' army, and the Siraki capital was destroyed. The Siraki king and Mithradates both surrendered. After this, history tells us very little about the Aorsi and Siraki. The Sarmatians

Opposite page: Roman soldiers behead captured Germans, allies of the Sarmatians during the Marcomannic Wars of the 160s and 170s.

to the west, on the other hand, gave Roman historians plenty of reasons to write about them.

WARS ALONG THE DANUBE

During the early decades of the first century CE, the Iazyges moved into the plains around the Tisza River, in what is now Hungary. We first hear of them in this area in 50 CE, when they became involved in a power struggle among Germanic tribes living to the north of them. The Iazyges allied with Vannius, a German king who had long enjoyed Roman support. Vannius was an unpopular tyrant, however, and many of his own people had joined with neighboring tribes to fight him.

As the conflict intensified, Vannius retreated into one of his fortresses, planning to hold out there. Unfortunately for him, wrote the historian Tacitus, his Iazyges horsemen "could not endure a siege [and] dispersed themselves throughout the surrounding countryside." Their activities provoked Vannius's enemies into all-out battle, so Vannius left his refuge and joined the fight. Defeated, he fled to the Danube. From there a Roman fleet took him and a large number of his followers to safety within the empire. The Iazyges, however, stayed behind, becoming even more firmly established around the Tisza.

By this time, the Roxolani had moved onto the steppe between the Carpathians and the Danube delta. When the Roman Empire exploded into civil war early in 69 CE, the Roxolani invaded the province of Moesia. They had already defeated two units of the Roman army and now, wrote Tacitus, "They had 9000 cavalry, flushed with victory and intent on plunder rather than on fighting." But the governor of Moesia was not as distracted by the civil war as the Roxolani had thought, and he sent the army after them:

> The Romans had everything ready for battle, the Sarmatians were scattered, and in their eagerness for plunder had encum-

bered themselves with heavy baggage, while the superior speed of their horses was lost on the slippery roads. . . . What with the continual slipping of their horses, and the weight of their coats of mail, they could make no use of their pikes or their swords, which being of an excessive length they wield with both hands. These coats are worn as defensive armour by the princes and most distinguished persons of the tribe . . . and though they are absolutely impenetrable to blows, yet they make it difficult for such as have been overthrown by the charge of the enemy to regain their feet. Besides, the Sarmatians were perpetually sinking in the deep and soft snow. The Roman soldier . . . continued to harass them with javelins and lances, and whenever the occasion required, closed with them with his short sword, and stabbed the defenceless enemy; for it is not their custom to defend themselves with a shield.

The Roxolani were subdued for the time being, but the Roman civil war raged on through the year. That autumn the general (soon to be emperor) Vespasian feared the border provinces were being left defenseless against possible barbarian threats. To deal with the danger, he recruited Iazyges leaders into his army. Tacitus tells us, "These chiefs also offered the services of their people, and its force of cavalry . . . but the offer was declined, lest . . . they should attempt some hostile enterprise, or, influenced by higher offers from other quarters, should cast off all sense of right and duty." Vespasian, like many Romans, had decided that although the Sarmatians had useful military skills, they were basically untrustworthy.

The emperor Vespasian reigned for ten years and restored order to Rome.

ENEMIES AND ALLIES

When Vespasian's son Domitian became emperor in 81, he was faced with a number of challenges from various barbarian groups. The most serious threat came from the Dacians, whose king Decebalus had been building up his army—and making alliances with the Sarmatians. In 85 he crossed the Danube to attack Moesia. Domitian responded by sending an expedition into Dacia. The fighting continued off and on until 92, when the Dacians and Sarmatians destroyed an entire Roman legion in the province of Pannonia (part of modern Hungary). An uneasy peace settlement was reached, with Decebalus making a show of submission to Rome and Rome making yearly payments to keep his loyalty.

By the turn of the century Rome had a new emperor, Trajan. He decided to go to war with the Dacians because, wrote ancient historian Cassius Dio, "he took into account their past deeds and was grieved at the amount of money they were receiving annually, and he also observed that their power and their pride were increasing." Trajan's first Dacian campaign was in 101–102, ending in a treaty. Defying the peace terms, Decebalus spent the next few years rebuilding his army and fortifications.

During this time, Cassius Dio tells us, Decebalus also made a point of "injuring those who had previously differed with him, even going so far as to annex a portion of the territory of the Iazyges." Although the Iazyges had opposed Domitian, they had sided with Trajan against Decebalus. The Roxolani, however, were still firmly allied with the Dacians. When Decebalus invaded Moesia in 105, Roxolani cavalry were part of his army. The Romans came to Moesia's rescue, and the next year Trajan went on the offensive. After having his men build a bridge over the Danube, he marched them across and fought his way to Sarmizegetusa.

As defeat became inevitable, Decebalus killed himself. Roman forces destroyed the Dacian capital, and Trajan claimed Dacia as a

Trajan had a tall marble column erected in Rome in celebration of his victories in Dacia. It is covered with scenes from the wars, including this one of men crossing the Danube.

Roman province—the first and only one north of the Danube. Then he made peace with the Roxolani, even accepting them as Roman allies. Soon after Trajan died, though, the Sarmatians broke the treaty.

In 117 the Roxolani attacked Moesia, while at the same time the Iazyges attacked Pannonia. The two Sarmatian tribes no doubt planned these actions together. Among other complaints, they were unhappy at being cut off from each other—evidently they were not allowed to travel freely back and forth through Dacia as they had done before it became a province. It took two years for the Romans to restore peace with the Sarmatians.

THE IAZYGES VS. MARCUS AURELIUS

War flared up again in the 160s, when several Germanic groups made forays into the empire. This began a series of conflicts known as the Marcomannic Wars, named after one of the leading German tribes, the Marcomanni. In 167 the Iazyges joined in on an invasion of Dacia, during which the province's governor was killed. The next year the

Marcus Aurelius's first love was philosophy, but he was forced to spend most of his reign fighting wars on the frontier. He belonged to the Stoic school of philosophy, which stressed the importance of good behavior and said that happiness was achieved by following reason and abstaining from passions.

emperor Marcus Aurelius began the empire's counterattack, but was able to accomplish little at first. In 169 the Iazyges killed the governor of Moesia in battle and defeated the legion he commanded. While the Romans battled the Iazyges, the Marcomanni and other German tribes crossed the Danube. When the Marcomanni reached Italy and besieged the city of Aquileia, Marcus Aurelius quickly arranged a treaty with the Iazyges so that he could turn his attention to the Germans.

The Iazyges bided their time till the winter of 173–174. Then they crossed the frozen Danube and once again invaded Pannonia. After engaging the Roman army, they headed back over the Danube. Cassius Dio, writing a couple decades later, describes what happened when they realized the Romans were pursuing them:

The Iazyges . . . awaited their opponents' onset, expecting to overcome them easily, as the others were not accustomed to the ice. Accordingly, some of the barbarians dashed straight at them, while others rode round to attack their flanks, as their horses had been trained to run safely even over a surface of this kind. The Romans upon observing this were not alarmed, but formed in a compact body, facing all their foes at once, and most of them laid down their shields and rested one foot upon them, so that they might not slip so much; and thus they received the enemy's charge. Some seized bridles, others the shields and spearshafts of their assailants, and drew the men toward them; and thus, becoming involved in close conflict, they knocked down both men and horses, since the barbarians by reason of their momentum could no longer keep from slipping. The Romans, to be sure, also slipped; but in case one of them fell on his back, he would drag his adversary down on top of him and then with his feet would hurl him backwards, as in a wrestling match.

The Iazyges were not used to this kind of fighting and lost the battle. In 174 their king Banadaspus offered to surrender to Marcus Aurelius, but the emperor turned him down—"because he knew their race to be untrustworthy and also because he . . . wished to annihilate them utterly," according to Cassius Dio. The Iazyges turned against Banadaspus and imprisoned him. Another high-ranking chief, Zanticus, took his place.

After another year of warfare, Marcus Aurelius may have felt he was close to finally defeating the Iazyges, when a rebellion arose in another part of the empire. So even though he really "wished to exterminate them utterly," he negotiated a treaty with Zanticus and the Iazyges commanders. The terms were strict. Among other provisions, the Iazyges were not allowed to live within ten miles of the Danube. Moreover, they were required to provide eight thousand horsemen to the Roman army. These men were split into a number of units and sent to far-off parts of the empire, including Britain and Egypt.

As for the Iazyges who remained, most of the restrictions on them were lifted in 179. They still were not allowed near the islands in the Danube, and they weren't permitted to own boats. They could visit and trade in marketplaces along the Danube on certain days. Most importantly, they were once more allowed to travel through Dacia to have dealings with the Roxolani—so long as they got the governor's permission first. For the time being, this was enough to keep things settled along the frontier.

NEW NOMADS

During all the upheavals along the Danube during the first and second centuries, a new group of Iranian-speaking nomads was gaining importance farther east. Known as the Alans (or Alani), they may have been closely related to the Sarmatians or have been a blending of eastern Sarmatians with other tribes. Their home territory was probably the steppe south of the Ural Mountains. By 60 CE they were also living north of the Caucasus and around the Sea of Azov and the Don River. In 72 they made the first of many extremely destructive raids on lands south of the Caucasus.

During the first two centuries CE the Alans caused trouble mostly for Persia. Greek and Roman writers mentioned them now and then, but not in great detail. Archaeologists, on the other hand, have been able to supply more information. The Alans' burials show both similarities to and differences from the Sarmatians and other Iranian-speaking nomads. The Alans buried their dead in small kurgans. In the eastern part of their territory there was usually only one person in each tomb, while farther west it was common for a tomb to hold two or more

OF THE 8,000 IAZYGES HORSEMEN ENROLLED IN THE ROMAN ARMY AS A RESULT OF Marcus Aurelius's treaty, 5,500 were sent to northern Britain. There they were broken up into units of 500 men each and stationed along Hadrian's Wall, which marked the boundary between Roman Britain and the unconquered part of the island (modern Scotland). When the Sarmatians finished their twenty-five-year terms of service, most of them probably settled down in the area near the wall, raising their families and training their sons in the arts of mounted warfare. It is likely that they also passed on their religious beliefs and practices, which were summarized by the historian Ammianus Marcellinus: "In their country is neither temple nor shrine, nor even thatched hut; only a naked sword stuck into the soil, which they worship with due reverence. Such is the war god who presides over the lands on which they wander." Some scholars think this may be the source of the legendary sword in the stone, which could only be drawn by the rightful king of Britain. There is also a theory that the king in the legend, Arthur, may have been a Sarmatian commander, or the descendant of one. Some of the earliest legends about King Arthur and his knights did in fact come from northern Britain, and the Sarmatians' presence there could certainly have influenced the region's people and their stories.

THE SWORD IN THE STONE

Did the stories of King Arthur have their source among the war-loving Sarmatians?

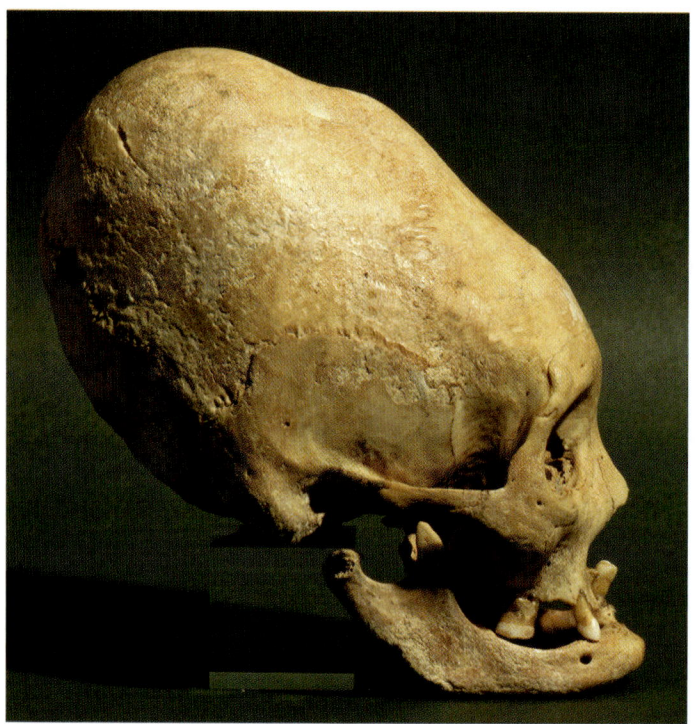

The artificially lengthened skull of a woman who died around 450 in what is now Germany. She appears to have been a lady of high rank among the Alans or Huns.

people. In Alan burials east of the Don River, many of the skeletons had artificially deformed skulls. This feature, shared a little later by Goths and Huns, was the result of carefully wrapping a baby's head in cloth to gradually lengthen it. We aren't sure exactly why this was done, but the procedure did not cause harm to the children's growth or intelligence.

Alan burials do not give us evidence that women served as warriors, as they did among some of the earlier nomad groups. This may be because the Alans did not use archery as much but focused on heavy cavalry warfare, which was best suited to large warriors with more upper body strength than most women could develop. The most common weapons found in Alan graves have been daggers and long swords. Arrows show up less frequently and are quite large, indicating that they were shot from longer bows than those used by the Scythians, Sauromatians, and Sarmatians.

During the early third century, a new people began to move into the Black Sea steppe. This was the Goths, a Germanic tribal confederation, which soon came to dominate the region between the Dnieper and the Don. Archaeologists have found no Sarmatian remains in this area that date to later than the middle of the third century. We don't know just what happened to the Black Sea Sarmatians. Probably many were killed in fighting the Goths, while others intermarried with the Goths and adopted Gothic culture, and still others moved west.

Soon a number of Goths were moving west, too, into the lands of the Roxolani on the lower Danube. By the 320s the Goths were so powerful in this region that it became known as Gothia. Most of the Roxolani, meanwhile, seem to have moved into Dacia and Iazyges territory. The upheaval among the Sarmatians provoked conflict with Rome. Historians wrote little about this time, but we do know that the emperor Galerius led a campaign against the Sarmatians during the first decade of the 300s.

In 323 the emperor Constantine went to war against Sarmatians who had crossed into the empire. Constantine won one battle against them in Pannonia, and another in Moesia. As part of the peace settlement, Constantine may have set up an alliance with the Sarmatians and recruited a number of their warriors into his army. In about 330, Sarmatians living between the Danube and the Tisza asked for Rome's help to stop the Goths from expanding into their lands. Constantine went to war against the Goths and was victorious. Then he again fought the Sarmatians, who seem to have broken their agreements with him. At some point between or after all these conflicts, Constantine settled large numbers of Iazyges as farmers in Pannonia. His feeling must have been that they were less of a threat inside the empire than outside it.

Meanwhile, the Alans continued to hold sway east of the Don—until the arrival of a new group of steppe nomads, the Huns. They were probably from Central Asia and probably spoke a language related to modern Turkish. Their mastery of horsemanship and archery was equal to that of the ancient Scythians. They were fast, fierce, and unstoppable. Hun warriors swept into the Alans' lands north of the Caucasus around 370. Then, "having traversed the territory of the Alani, and having slain many of them and acquired much plunder, [the Huns] made a treaty of friendship and alliance with those who remained."

After this, the story of horse-riding nomads in Europe belongs mainly to the Huns, who conquered all of the Sarmatians north of the Danube. The independent history of the Alans, however, was not quite over. In the early 400s most of the Alans broke away from the Huns and migrated into western Europe. Banding together with the Vandals, a Germanic people, they invaded what are now France and Spain. Then in 439 the two peoples headed south and conquered the Roman Empire's provinces in North Africa. They ruled there till 534, when imperial forces retook the provinces.

Alans still remained north of the Caucasus, eventually settling down to live by farming and raising livestock. They built up a kingdom that had political and cultural ties to other states in the region and became very prosperous. An Arab historian wrote this description in the tenth century: "The Alan king [can] muster 30,000 horsemen. He is powerful, very strong and influential [among] the kings. The kingdom consists of an uninterrupted series of settlements; when the cock crows [in one of them], the answer comes from the other parts of the kingdom, because the villages are intermingled and close together." The modern descendants of the Alans live in the Ossetia region of Georgia and southern Russia.

The Alans (and Sarmatians) lived on in a different way, too. Many of the peoples they encountered—Persians, Romans, Goths, and others—were so impressed by the nomads' heavy cavalry that they added such forces to their own armies. Oftentimes they recruited Sarmatian or Alan horsemen, but they also trained and equipped their own mounted soldiers with lances and heavy armor. After the Roman Empire ended in western Europe, cavalry warriors like these played a major role not only in warfare but in government and other aspects of society. They came to be known as knights, and they are still with us, in our history, legends, books, movies, and imaginations.

THE ALANS

LATE IN THE FOURTH CENTURY, A RETIRED ROMAN SOLDIER NAMED AMMIANUS Marcellinus set out to write a history of the Roman Empire from the first century to his own time. He composed the final volume in around 390. In it he recalled the turmoil that accompanied the rise of the Huns, and included this description of their allies the Alans:

> They have no cottages, and never use the plough, but live solely on meat and plenty of milk, mounted on their waggons, which they cover with a curved awning made of the bark of trees, and then drive them through their boundless [plains]. And when they come to any pasture land, they pitch their waggons in a circle. . . . These waggons, in short, are their perpetual habitation, and wherever they fix them, that place they look upon as their home.
>
> They drive before them their flocks and herds to their pasturage; and, above all other [livestock], they are especially careful of their horses. . . . All their old people, and especially the weak, keep close to the waggons, and occupy themselves in the lighter employments. But the young men, who from their earliest childhood are trained to the use of horses, think it beneath them to walk. They are also all trained by careful discipline of various sorts to become skillful warriors. . . . Nearly all the Alani men are of great stature and beauty; their hair is somewhat yellow, their eyes are terribly fierce. . . . And as ease is a delightful thing to men of a quiet and placid disposition, so danger and war are a pleasure to the Alani, and among them that man is called happy who has lost his life in battle. . . . They have no idea of slavery, inasmuch as they themselves are all born of noble families; and those whom even now they appoint to be judges are always men of proved experience and skill in war.

Above: This figure, knees bent in riding posture, was discovered in an ancient cemetery in the Crimea, where both Goths and Alans lived.

Key Dates in Scythian and Sarmatian History

eighth—third centuries BCE Sakas occupy eastern steppes, Tien Shan, and Altai Mountains

late eighth century BCE Scythians move into Caucasus region

around 678 BCE Scythian king Ishpakai attacks Assyrian Empire

around 674 BCE Scythian king Bartatua marries Assyrian princess

around 610 BCE Scythians and Medes conquer Nineveh; Medes then push Scythians back to north of Caucasus

late seventh century BCE founding of Belsk on a tributary of the Dnieper

sixth—fifth centuries BCE Sauromatians occupy steppes between Don and Volga rivers and south of Urals

530 BCE Massagetae led by Tomyris defeat Cyrus the Great

520 BCE Darius I's victory over the "pointed-hat" Sakas

513 BCE Darius I's expedition against Scythians north of Black Sea

around 450 BCE Herodotus's visit to Black Sea town of Olbia

fourth century BCE Sarmatians move into Sauromatian territory

339 BCE Philip II of Macedonia defeats Scythian king Ateas

331 BCE Scythians destroy Macedonian army north of the Black Sea

A foot long, this golden stag decorated a Scythian warrior's shield.

329 BCE Alexander the Great fights Sakas in Central Asia

late third century BCE Scythian center of power shifts to Crimea

by 200 BCE Sarmatians dominate Black Sea steppe

78—76 BCE Roman expedition against Iazyges north of the Danube

6 CE Iazyges raid Roman territory south of the Danube

8 CE Roman poet Ovid banished to Tomis on the Black Sea

49 CE Sarmatians involved on both sides of civil war in Crimea

60s CE Alans living north of Caucasus and around Don River and Sea of Azov

69 CE Roxolani invade Moesia; Iazyges leaders recruited in Roman civil war

72 CE Alans raid south of the Caucasus

85—92 CE Sarmatians fight with Dacians against Domitian

101—102, 105—106 CE Trajan's Dacian wars

117—119 CE uprising of Iazyges and Roxolani

166—180 CE Marcomannic Wars

175 CE peace treaty requires 8,000 Iazyges to serve in Roman army

200s CE Sarmatians north of Black Sea displaced by Goths

323 CE Constantine campaigns against the Sarmatians

around 330 CE Constantine campaigns against Goths in Sarmatian territory

around 370 CE Huns conquer Alans, who become Hun allies

406 CE Alans, Vandals, and other barbarians invade what is now France

439 CE Alans and Vandals conquer North Africa

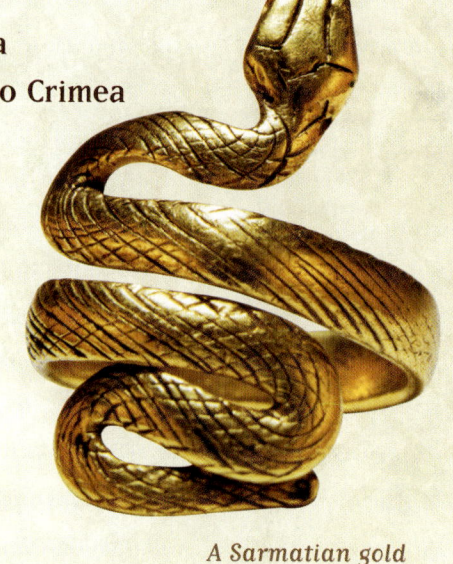

A Sarmatian gold ring, formed in the shape of a snake

A Scythian gold ring from the fifth century BCE

GLOSSARY

amulet An object worn or carried to ward off evil or bring good luck, strength, or other desirable qualities.

Asia Minor A large peninsula surrounded by the Mediterranean, Aegean, and Black seas. Also called Anatolia, it is the part of modern Turkey that lies in Asia.

Balkan Peninsula A peninsula surrounded by the Adriatic, Mediterranean, Aegean, and Black seas. Today it is occupied by the nations of Greece, Macedonia, Albania, Bosnia, Croatia, Slovenia, Yugoslavia, Bulgaria, part of Romania, and the European portion of Turkey.

cavalry Soldiers who fought on horseback.

divination Practices that seek to discover hidden knowledge about the past, present, or future.

Germanic A language family that includes German, Dutch, English, Danish, Norwegian, and Swedish; can also refer to peoples who spoke Germanic languages and to their culture.

infantry Soldiers who fought on foot.

Iranian A language family that includes Persian (or Farsi), Pashtun (a language of Afghanistan), and Ossetic (a descendant of the Alans' language, now spoken in parts of Georgia and southern Russia).

koumiss Fermented mare's milk, slightly alcoholic and high in vitamin C and other nutrients.

mercenaries Soldiers who hire out their services to anyone willing to pay.

Pannonia The Roman name for the part of Hungary west and south of the Danube River.

FOR MORE INFORMATION

BOOKS

Brzezinski, Richard, and Mariusz Mielczarek. *The Sarmatians 600 BC–AD 450.* Oxford: Osprey Publishing, 2002.

Buell, Janet. *Ancient Horsemen of Siberia.* Minneapolis, MN: Twenty-First Century Books, 1998.

Cernenko, E. V. *Scythians 700–300 B.C.* Oxford: Osprey Publishing, 1983.

Whiting, Jim. *The Life and Times of Herodotus.* Hockessin, DE: Mitchell Lane Publishers, 2006.

WEB SITES

BBC/WGBH. *Nova.* "Ice Mummies: Siberian Ice Maiden."
  http://www.pbs.org/wgbh/nova/transcripts/2517siberian.html

Center for the Study of Eurasian Nomads.
  http://www.csen.org/

Department of Art History, University of Pittsburgh. *Scythian Slide Collection.*
  http://www.pitt.edu/~haskins/

Educational Broadcasting Corporation. *Secrets of the Dead.* "Amazon Warrior Women."
  http://www.pbs.org/wnet/secrets/previous_seasons/case_amazon/index.html

SELECTED BIBLIOGRAPHY

Cassius Dio. *Roman History.* Translated by Earnest Cary. Online at http://penelope.uchicago.edu/Thayer/E/Roman/Texts/Cassius_Dio/home.html

Cunliffe, Barry, ed. *Prehistoric Europe: An Illustrated History.* New York: Oxford University Press, 1994.

Davis-Kimball, Jeannine. *Warrior Women: An Archaeologist's Search for History's Hidden Heroines.* New York: Warner Books, 2002.

Davis-Kimball, Jeannine, Vladimir A. Bashilov, and Leonid T. Yablonsky, eds. *Nomads of the Eurasian Steppes in the Early Iron Age.* Berkeley, CA: Zinat Press, 1995.

Diodorus Siculus. *Library of History.* Translated by C. H. Oldfather et al. Online at http://penelope.uchicago.edu/Thayer/E/Roman/Texts/Diodorus_Siculus/home.html

Frye, Richard N. *The Heritage of Central Asia: From Antiquity to the Turkish Expansion.* Princeton: Markus Wiener, 1996.

Herodotus. *The Histories.* Translated by A. D. Godley. Online at http://www.perseus.tufts.edu/cgi-bin/ptext?lookup=Hdt.+toc

Hildinger, Erik. *Warriors of the Steppe: A Military History of Central Asia, 500 B.C. to 1700 A.D.* New York: Sarpedon, 1997.

McCullough, David Willis, ed. *Chronicles of the Barbarians: Firsthand Accounts of Pillage and Conquest, From the Ancient World to the Fall of Constantinople.* New York: Times Books, 1998.

Rolle, Renate. *The World of the Scythians.* Translated by F. G. Walls. Berkeley: University of California Press, 1989.

Tacitus. *The Annals.* Translated by Alfred John Church and William Jackson Brodribb. Online at http://www.perseus.tufts.edu/cgi-bin/ptext?lookup=Tac.+Ann.+toc

———. *The History.* Translated by Alfred John Church and William

Jackson Brodribb. Online at http://www.perseus.tufts.edu/cgi-bin/ptext?lookup=Tac.+Hist.+toc

Trippett, Frank, and the Editors of Time-Life Books. *The First Horsemen.* New York: Time-Life Books, 1974.

Wilde, Lyn Webster. *On the Trail of the Women Warriors: The Amazons in Myth and History.* New York: St. Martin's Press, 2000.

Williams, Derek. *Romans and Barbarians: Four Views from the Empire's Edge.* New York: St. Martin's Press, 1998.

SOURCES FOR QUOTATIONS

Chapter 1

p. 10 "Would you like": Williams, *Romans and Barbarians*, p. 46.

p. 11 "One sees nothing": Rolle, *The World of the Scythians*, p. 17.

p. 14 "mare-milking Scythians": Cunliffe, *Prehistoric Europe*, p. 388.

p. 15 "Behold, a people": Davis-Kimball, *Warrior Women*, p. 51.

p. 15 "and the whole land": Herodotus, *The Histories* 1.106.

p. 16 "when the Scythians": ibid. 4.1.

p. 16 "Men of Scythia": ibid. 4.3.

p. 17 "the flying metal" and "a double death": Rolle, *The World of the Scythians*, p. 65.

Chapter 2

p. 20 "like the Scythians": Herodotus, *The Histories* 1.215.

p. 20 "Stop hurrying": ibid. 1.206.

p. 21 "Do not be elated": ibid. 1.212.

p. 21 "Tomyris, when Cyrus": ibid. 1.214.

p. 22 "I went to Saka land": Frye, *The Heritage of Central Asia*, p. 83.

p. 23 "The Scythians sent": Herodotus, *The Histories* 4.121.

p. 25 "You crazy man": ibid. 4.126.

p. 25 "Persian, such is": Rolle, *The World of the Scythians*, p. 59.

p. 25 "The Persians asked": Herodotus, *The Histories* 4.131.

p. 25 "Unless you become birds": ibid. 4.132.

p. 25 "After sending the gifts": ibid. 4.134.

p. 27 "As to masters": ibid. 4.127.

Chapter 3

p. 29 "Though in most respects": Hildinger, *Warriors of the Steppe*, pp. 36–37.

p. 31 "As for giving": Herodotus, *The Histories* 4.70.

p. 32 "gave them the art": ibid. 4.67.

p. 32 "They bring great bundles": ibid. 4.67.

p. 32 "A Scythian drinks": ibid. 4.64–65.

p. 33 "They take the king's": Trippett, *The First Horsemen*, p. 118.

p. 33 "There the body": ibid., p. 121.

p. 33 "they take the most": Herodotus, *The Histories* 4.72.

p. 38 "One was a young woman" and "may have led": Wilde, *On the Trail of the Women Warriors*, p. 49.

p. 38 "there came in Scythia": Diodorus Siculus, *Library of History* 2.44.1.

p. 39 "The women of the Sauromatae": Herodotus, *The Histories* 4.116–117.

p. 39 "A woman who takes": Wilde, *On the Trail of the Women Warriors*, p. 43.

Chapter 4

p. 46 "gave his daughter": Davis-Kimball, *Nomads of the Eurasian Steppes*, p. 73.

p. 47 "Anacharsis said": Rolle, *The World of the Scythians*, p. 129.

p. 48 "This people became": Diodorus Siculus, *Library of History* 2.43.7.

p. 48 "They turn over": Williams, *Romans and Barbarians*, p. 50.

p. 48 "The line of battle": ibid., p. 50.

p. 49 "[The Sarmatians] collect": Hildinger, *Warriors of the Steppe*, p. 48.

p. 51 "While summer lasts": Williams, *Romans and Barbarians*, p. 52.

p. 51 "When Danube by the north": ibid., p. 53.

p. 52 "Some flee": ibid., pp. 53–54.

p. 53 "Now are the frighted": ibid., pp. 55–56.

Chapter 5

p. 56 "could not endure": Tacitus, *Annals* 12.30.

p. 56 "They had 9000" and "The Romans had everything": Tacitus, *History* 1.79.

p. 57 "These chiefs also": ibid. 3.5.

p. 58 "he took into account": Cassius Dio, *Roman History* 68.6.

p. 58 "injuring those who": ibid. 68.10.

p. 61 "The Iazyges . . . awaited": ibid. 72.7.

p. 61 "because he knew": ibid. 72.13.

p. 61 "wished to exterminate": ibid. 72.16.

p. 63 "In their country": Williams, *Romans and Barbarians*, p. 48.

p. 65 "having traversed": McCullough, *Chronicles of the Barbarians*, p. 125.

p. 66 "The Alan king": "Alans" in *Encyclopaedia Iranica*, online at http://www.iranica.com/newsite

p. 67 "They have no cottages": McCullough, *Chronicles of the Barbarians*, pp. 124–125.

INDEX

Page numbers for illustrations are in boldface

Map, 24

Alans (nomads), 62, 64–67, **64**, **67**
Alexander the Great, 45
Ammianus Marcellinus (historian), 63, 67
Anacharsis (sage), 47
Aorsi (Sarmatian tribe), 49, 50, 55
archery, 12–13, **13**, 14, **14**, 17, **17**, 48
Arthur legend, King, 63, **63**
Assyrian Empire, 15
Ateas (Scythian king), 43–44
Augustus (emperor), 9

Banadaspus (Iazyges king), 61
Bartatua (Scythian chief), 15
Black Sea, 9, 10, 15, 23, 43, 45, 46, 48, 64
burial customs
   Alans, 62, 64, **64**
   Scythian, 33–37, **33**, **34**, **35**, **37**

Cassius Dio (historian), 58, 60–61
Caucasus Mountains, 15, 16

centaurs, 14, **14**
Cimmerians, 15
Constantine (emperor), 65
craftspeople, 31, **31**, 33, **33**
Crimean Scythians, 45–46
Croesus (ruler of Lydia), 47
Cyrus the Great, 19, 20–22

Dacians, 50–51, 58–59
Danube River, 23, 43, 44, 50, 51, 56, 60, 61
Darius I, **18**, 22, **22**, 23, 25, 26, 29–30
Davis-Kimball, Jeannine (archaeologist), 39–40, 41
Decebalus (Dacian king), 58
Diodorus Siculus (historian), 38, 47, 48
divination/diviners, 32
Dnieper River, 30, 32, 50, 64
Domitian (emperor), 58
Don River, 23, 25, 43, 46, 49, 50, 62, 64, 65

Enarees (diviners), 32

farms, steppe farmland, 11–12, **12**

Galerius (emperor), 65

German tribes, 59–60
Getans (barbarians), 9, 44–45
gods and goddesses, 27
gold, **27**, **28**, 31, **31**, **41**, **42**, **47**, **69**
Gothia, 65
Goths, 46, 64–65
Greek and Scythian culture, 30–31, **31**

Hadrian's Wall, 63
Herodotus (historian), **30**
   and Greek and Scythian culture, 30–31, 32–33, 34, 39
   invasion of Scythia, 23, 25–26, 29–30
   on Massagetae peoples, 20, 21–22
   Scythian death customs, 32–33, 34, 37
   on Scythian gods and goddesses, 27
   on Scythians in the Middle East, 15, 16
Hesiod (author), 14
horsemanship, 10, 11–12, 65
   horse burials, 35, **35**, 37
   horses as spiritual symbol, 27, **27**
   nomad horse archers, 12–13, **13**, 14, **14**, 17, 48

Huns, 46, 64, 65

Iazyges (barbarians), 50–51, 56, 57, 58, 59–62
Idanthyrsus (Scythian ruler), 23, 25, 27
Ishpakai (Scythian chief), 15

Jeremiah (prophet), 15

King Arthur legend, 63, **63**
knights, 66
kurgans (burial mounds), 34–38, **34**, **35**

language, 9, 19

Madyes (Scythian chief), 15
Marcomannic Wars, **54**, 59–62, **60**
Marcus Aurelius (emperor), 60–62, **60**
Massagetae people, 20–22, **21**
Medes, 15, 16
metalworkers, Scythian, 31
Mithradates (Greek king), 55
Mithradates the Great, 45–46, **46**, 50

nomadic pastoralism, 12

INDEX

nomads, steppe, 10–13, **12**, 14

Ovid (poet), 9–10, **10**, 51–53

pastoralism, 12
Pausanias (historian), 48–49
Persian Empire, **18**, 19, 20, 23, 25, 45
Phillip II of Macedonia, 44–45, **44**
poetry, 9–10, **10**, 51–53, **52**

religion, Scythian, 27, **27**
Rolle, Renate (archaeologist), 38
Roman Empire, 46, **54**, 55
  end of, 66
  Iazyges vs. Marcus Aurelius, 59–62, **60**
  Roman civil war, 56–59, **57**
  Sarmatians migration and, 50–51
Roxolani (Sarmatian tribe), 45, 50, 51, 56–57, 58, 59, 62, 64–65

Sakas (nomad horse archers), 19–20, **20**, 45
Sauromatians, 23, 25, 38–39, 43, 46
Scythia
  golden age, 43–44
  invasion of, 23, 25–26, 29–30
Scythians and Sarmatians, 9–10, 46
  early Sarmatian culture, 39–40
  early Scythian encounters, 13, 15–16
  funeral and burial customs, 33–37, **33**, **34**, **35**, **37**
  key dates, 68–69
  prophecy and divination, 32
  religion, 27, **27**
  Sakas, 19–22, **20**
  Sarmatian conflicts, **54**, 55–59, **57**
  Sarmatians and King Arthur legend, 63, **63**
  Sarmatians migration, 46, 48–53, **49**
  Scythian and Greek culture, 30–31, **31**
  Scythian last stands, 43–46
  Scythian warriors, **8**, 15–16, 17, **17**, 36, 38–40, **38**, **39**
  Scythians as real centaurs, 14, **14**
  as steppe peoples, 10–13, **12**
  vows of loyalty, **28**, 31–32
  world of, **24**
Sea of Azov, 55, 62

Seven Sages, 47
Siraki (Sarmatian tribe), 49, 50, 55
steppes, Eurasian, 10–13, **12**
Strabo (geographer), 48

Tacitus (historian), 48, 56, 57
Thrace, 23
Tisza River, 56
tombs, 34–37
Tomyris (Massagetae queen), 20–22, **21**
Trajan (emperor), 58–59, **59**

Vandals, 66
Vannius (German king), 56
Vespasian (emperor), 57, **57**

Volga River, 46

warfare and military skills
    Alan warriors, 64
    bows and arrows, 17, **17**
    customs related to warfare, 32
    mounted archery, 12–13, **13**, 48
    Sarmatian warriors, 48–49, **49**
    Scythian warriors, 15–16, 17, **17**, 36, 38–40, **38**, **39**
women, Scythian, 16, 44, 46
    priestesses, 40, 41, **41**
    women warriors, 36, 38–40, **38**, **39**

Zanticus (Iazyges king), 61

INDEX   79

ABOUT THE AUTHOR

Kathryn Hinds grew up near Rochester, New York. She studied music and writing at Barnard College, and went on to do graduate work in comparative literature and medieval studies at the City University of New York. She has written more than forty books for young people, including *Everyday Life in Medieval Europe* and the books in the series LIFE IN THE MEDIEVAL MUSLIM WORLD, LIFE IN ELIZABETHAN ENGLAND, LIFE IN ANCIENT EGYPT, LIFE IN THE ROMAN EMPIRE, and LIFE IN THE RENAISSANCE. Kathryn lives in the north Georgia mountains with her husband, their son, and an assortment of cats and dogs. When she is not reading or writing, she enjoys dancing, gardening, knitting, playing music, and taking walks in the woods. Visit Kathryn online at www.kathrynhinds.com